Liberty at Risk

Other Books by Gary DeMar

Liberty at Risk

EXPOSING THE POLITICS OF PLUNDER

Gary DeMar

American Vision
Powder Springs, Georgia

ISBN: 0–915815–44–3

Printed in the United States of America

03 04 05 06   6 5 4 3 2 1

For further information about American Vision, visit our website at

www.americanvision.org

or write: American Vision, 3150-A Florence Rd.,
           Powder Springs, Georgia 30127
           or call 1-800–628–9460

Table of Contents

Introduction

W hen my oldest son was about four, we were at the check-out line at a Blockbuster video store when he noticed a videotape display promoting the newly released *Godfather* trilogy on video tape. "Dad, are these movies about God?" he asked. A reasonable question for a four-year-old given the title and his incessant questions about everything. Knowing that he would not care to hear a long retelling of the plot, I summed up the storyline by telling him that *The Godfather* saga was about an alternate form of government. The man standing behind us in line overheard our conversation and made the following comment. "I never thought of it that way, but you're right. Don Corleone is a lot like today's politicians. He's the man in charge. He grants political favors. He makes and enforces laws. He even collects taxes. The Mafia[1] is run like a government."

Five Points of Government

Vito Corleone began his crime-boss career by working outside the political system and the conventions of morality and law by developing a parallel but counterfeit government. His organization and his governing principles had the five necessary characteristics that make up a functioning governmental structure:

1. **Sovereignty:** Who's in charge? (Don Vito Corleone.)
2. **Hierarchy:** To whom do I report? (Clemenza, Tesio, "buffers.")
3. **Law:** What are the rules? (Don't go against "the family.")

4. **Positive and Negative Sanctions**: What happens if I keep/break the rules? (**Positive sanctions**: advancement, a piece of the action, your own "family": **Negative sanctions**: bullet in the eye, bullet in the back of the head, bullet in the front of the head, horse head in your bed, strangulation, sleep with the fishes.)

5. **Continuity**: Is there a future? (Maintain and perpetuate "the family" at all costs.)

The government of the Godfather lacked one thing: legitimacy, the most important factor in establishing confidence, continuity, liberty, and justice in any form of government. But even without legal legitimacy, the Godfather's government worked at various levels because it supplied a service to the community. It dealt with heavy-handed criminal rivals, solved problems for the politically disconnected, and granted favors to the dissatisfied, disillusioned, and disenfranchised. People turned to the Godfather out of hopelessness. For these people, the government of the Godfather was considered salvific. The Don was seen as a benevolent dictator. In reality, the Godfather's government was the exercise of raw and unregulated power with the claim that it was for the good of the people and the community.

Seeking Justice

In the movie's opening scene, Amerigo Bonasera, a patriotic and loyal Italian American, tells Don Corleone how he and his wife sat in a New York Criminal Court room and watched as they saw justice slip away from them. The judge described Bonasera's daughter's attackers as "the worst kind of degenerates. . . wild beasts." Amerigo agreed, muttering "*animales*" under his breath. They had savagely beaten his daughter in their failed attempt to rape her, nearly killing her in the process. But then he heard the words: "Suspended sentence." The judge had let them go. No punishment. No justice. No satisfaction. Bonasera swore vengeance. But how? Mario Puzo, author of the best-selling *Godfather* novel, describes what happens next:

All his years in America, Amerigo Bonasera had trusted in law and order. And he prospered thereby. Now, though his brain smoked with hatred, though wild visions of buying a gun and killing the two young men jangled the very bones of his skull, Bonasera turned to his still uncomprehending wife and explained to her, "They have made fools of us." He paused and then made his decision, no longer fearing the cost. "For justice we must go on our knees to Don Corleone."[2]

Bonasera's desperation sets the tone for the rest of the book and movie and encapsulates the meaning of the Godfather's governmental role. "Francis Ford Coppola and Puzo understood the need to show the alternate moral universe of the mafia,"[3] a competing and somewhat competent governmental organization with religious overtones. The Godfather was a sacred yet unofficial position in the community. It would take the humbled position of penitents—"on their knees" they approach—to seek his forgiveness for not coming to him first as the true dispenser of justice. The goal of the Godfather is for the undertaker to change his loyalty from the government that betrayed him to the only government that can save him. Paul Rahe's comments are significant:

> In his novel, Puzo brings this home to his readers by conferring on the undertaker the name "Amerigo," that of the Italian after whom America was named, and by giving him the surname "Bonasera," which is Italian for "Good night." In agreeing to accept Don Corleone's "gift" and to become his "friend," Amerigo Bonasera says "good night" to America. In pondering this even, we may wish to reflect on the fact that in German *Gift* is the word for poison.[4]

The Godfather's government was considered to be good by so many because it granted favors, dispensing what many wanted to believe was justice when it could not be obtained in city courts or the streets. Legitimacy was not an immediate issue as long as the people received a benefit and general good was being performed, give or take a few broken legs. Those under the counterfeit jurisdiction of the Don's regime were willing to put up with paying extorted "protection money," since most people understood the costs involved in running a government, even legitimate governments. They considered it a tax for promised services.

"For the Good of the People"

The Godfather bought off police officers, politicians, and judges to amass power and extend the jurisdiction of his Family's influence, all for the good of the people and the community. Those holding legitimate governmental positions benefitted as well with financial kickbacks. The Don's "cabinet officers" were uncompromisingly loyal. His wife was equally loyal and unquestioning of his methods. The Don never directly involved himself in implementing his corrupt but effective policies. He hired "buffers," underlings, to carry out his edicts. An empire was created outside the law but with the protection of the law.

Don Corleone protected his interests by crushing any person or competing crime family that opposed his will. It wasn't personal; it was business. Each recipient of the Don's favor would carry a lifetime debt that one day might have to be repaid. And there were many people in his debt. Loyalty was rewarded; disloyalty was severely punished. The Godfather was a political predator masquerading as a benevolent governor of the people. The family business (government) had to be protected at all costs. Legacies were important. Power from the Don was passed on to the most competent son, insuring the future of the family.

"Government Policy"

The predatory politics and violent methods of the Godfather are criminal. Everyone understands this. But what is considered criminal when practiced by the Godfather, all of a sudden becomes "government policy" in legislation coming from Washington. Lavish government spending programs and burdensome tax bills are legitimized by describing them as just, benevolent, fair, and good for the people. The rule of law (the Constitution) is often ignored and most often subverted to gain political power at the expense of personal freedom and liberty. Wealth is confiscated from the productive and transferred to the less productive in an attempt to buy votes. Vote buying becomes a means of increasing the scope of governmental power and legitimizes policies that can find no constitutional justification. As long as those in power offer the benefits that come with power, few people complain, except, of course, those who are being fleeced with ever-growing tax bills.

Without a proper understanding of the State's biblical and constitutional purpose, function, and jurisdiction Christians can be trapped into believing that the State ought to promote policies beyond its legitimate role and authority as long as it is all for "the good of the people." This can lead some to turn to the State for security at any cost to freedom. In the development of his own social and political goals, Adolf Hitler studied the policies of Otto Von Bismark because Bismark understood the German state of mind. Hitler remarks in *Mein Kampf:* "I studied Bismark's socialist legislation in its intention, struggle and success." William L. Shirer, author of *The Rise and Fall of the Third Reich,* observes: "To combat socialism Bismark put through between 1883 and 1889 a program for social security far beyond anything known in other countries. It included compulsory insurance for workers against old age, sickness, accident and incapacity, and though organized by the State it was financed by employers and employees. It cannot be said that it stopped the rise of the Social Democrats or the trade unions, but it did have a profound influence on the working class *in that it gradually made them value security over political freedom and caused them to see in the State, however conservative, a benefactor and a protector.*"[5]

The Idol State

While the extremes of Hitler's regime may seem like a radical comparison, there is much about our own social and political condition that should worry us. Herbert Schlossberg's masterful study of power in his book *Idols for Destruction* is both prophetic and frightening:

> Rulers have ever been tempted to play the role of father to
> their people. . . . The state that acts like a wise parent instead of
> a vindictive judge has been an attractive image to many people.
> They include ecclesiastical authorities who have completely misses
> the point of the gospel warning to "call no man your father on
> earth, for you have one Father, who is in heaven" (Matt. 23:9).
> The father is the symbol not only of authority but also of provi-
> sion. "Our Father who art in heaven. . . . Give us this day our
> daily bread" (Matt. 6:9, 11). Looking to the state for sustenance
> is a cultic act [an act of worship]; we rightly learn to expect food
> from parents, and when we regard the state as the source of physi-
> cal provision we render to it the obeisance of idolatry. The crowds
> who had fed on the multiplied loaves and fishes were ready to
> receive Christ as their ruler, not because of who he was but be-
> cause of the provision. John Howard Yoder[6] has rightly inter-
> preted that scene: "The distribution of bread moved the crowd
> to acclaim Jesus as the new Moses, the provider, the Welfare
> King whom they had been waiting for."[7]

Power can become most dangerous in the hands of good people,
because they believe their intentions to help the less fortunate are righteous and just. Jesus used His vast abilities sparingly. He did not issue a
call to plunder the rich to pay for the needs of the poor. Few people today
understand the danger of power, even in the hands of the righteous who
want to do good things with it. In J. R. R. Tolkien's *The Lord of the Rings*,
the power of the ring is not something to be desired even by good people.
The goal is to destroy it. When Boromir fails to avoid the ring's power, he
dies. Even Gandalf and the elves shun the power of the ring. Tolkien is
doubtful that any person has the ability to resist the temptation of absolute power promised by the ring, even if that power is used for good. That
is one of the great themes of the series. Schlossberg continues:

The paternal state not only feeds its children, but nurtures, educates, comforts, and disciplines them, providing all they need for their security. This appears to be a mildly insulting way to treat adults, but it is really a great crime because it transforms the state from being a gift of God, given to protect us against violence, into an idol. It supplies us with all blessings, and we look to it for all our needs. Once we sink to that level, as [C.S.] Lewis says, there is no point in telling state officials to mind their own business. "Our whole lives *are* their business."[8] The paternalism of the state is that of the bad parent who wants his children dependent on him forever. That is an evil impulse. The good parent prepares his children for independence, trains them to make responsible decisions, knows that he harms them by not helping them to break loose. The paternal state thrives on dependency. When the dependents free themselves, it loses power. It is, therefore, parasitic on the very persons whom it turns into parasites. Thus, the state and its dependents march symbiotically [in close union with one another] to destruction.[9]

Once the State gains power, it works relentlessly to maintain power. Since it gained power by promising the masses security, it must offer more security to maintain and gain more power. The time will come when promises cannot be kept because the productive members of society have been plundered of their ability to create wealth. The incentive to work, create, and profit from their labor has been destroyed.

When the provision of paternal security replaces the provision of justice as the function of the state, the state stops providing justice. The ersatz [artificial and inferior substitute] parent ceases executing judgment against those who violate the law, and the nation begins losing benefits of justice. Those who are concerned about the chaos into which the criminal justice system has fallen should consider what the state's function has become. Because the state can only be a bad imitation of a father, as a dancing bear act is of a ballerina, the protection of this Leviathan of a father turns out to be a bear hug.[10]

Politicians pick up on the desire for security and dependency and use it for permanent political gain: "The idol state uses the language of compassion because its intention is a messianic one. It finds the masses harassed and helpless, like sheep without a shepherd, needing a savior."[11]

Paved with Good Intentions

The intention to do good becomes a destructive force when it keeps people in a condition of dependency. When George W. Bush proposed a tax cut for all wage earners in 2003, Alan M. Webber, founding editor of *Fast Company* magazine, presented the classic plunder-to-satisfy-the-wants-of-the-people worldview. "At the community level," he writes, "ordinary folks want jobs, they want benefits, and they want reassurance. This is the time, not for tax cuts, but for Democratic-style spending programs: temporary job creation, targeted public works expenditures, extended unemployment benefits."[12] Webber believes that confiscating money from wage earners, passing it through a huge bureaucracy, and then distributing a lesser amount of money to the helpless masses is better than allowing wage earners to keep their money, save it, spend it, and invest it, thereby making money less expensive to borrow and accessible for investment to everyone.

Real jobs are created, and fewer people remain dependent on the State when consumers make their own economic decisions. Webber believes that a complex and multifaceted economy is better managed by bureaucrats than by people who actually make countless specialized and personal economic decisions every day. The only ones who benefit by "public works expenditures" are the politicians who create the programs and those empowered to implement them. The losers are the productive members of society who are plundered and those who become dependent on confiscated wealth given to them in the name of compassion.

*　*　*　*　*

The majority of Americans do not understand the basic principles of government, especially as they relate to *civil* government. Even Christians are often ignorant of basic biblical principles related to how governments should function The chapters that follow are designed to put the role of government at all levels in biblical, historical, and practical perspective. Government is not evil. When practiced with wisdom and the restraints of a Constitution limiting its power to be an all-granting benefactor, the result is true freedom under God.

Notes

1. "Family" was substituted for "Mafia" in *The Godfather* so as not to offend Italian-Americans.

2. Mario Puzo, *The Godfather* (New York: G. P. Putnam's Sons, 1969), 12.

3. Jonah Goldberg, "Goodnight America: What Loving the Mob Really Means," *National Review Online* (March 5, 2001), www.nationalreview.com/goldberg/goldberg030501.shtml

4. Paul Rahe, "Don Corleone, Multiculturalist," *The Journal of Business and Professional Ethics*, 16:1–3 (1998), 137. An earlier version of this article was published as "Don Vito Corleone, Friendship, and the American Regime" in *Reinventing the American People: Unity and Diversity Today*, ed. Robert Royal (Washington, D.C.: Ethics and Public Policy Center, 1995), 115–135.

5. William Shirer, *The Rise and Fall of the Third Reich* (New York, NY: Simon and Schuster, 1960), 96.

6. John Howard Yoder, *The Politics of Jesus: Vicit Angus Noster*, 2nd ed. (Grand Rapids, MI: Eerdmans, [1972] 1994), 34–35.

7. Herbert Schlossberg, *Idols for Destruction: The Conflict of Christian Faith and American Culture* (Wheaton, IL: Crossway Books, [1983] 1993), 183.

8. C.S. Lewis, *God in the Dock*, ed. Walter Hooper (Grand Rapids, MI: Eerdmans, 1970), 314.

9. Schlossberg, *Idols for Destruction*, 184.

10. Schlossberg, *Idols for Destruction*, 184.

11. Schlossberg, *Idols for Destruction*, 185.

12. Alan M. Webber, "Bush's proposed tax cuts won't rescue sinking U.S. economy," *USA Today* (January 13, 2003), 13A.

Part One

God is Ultimately Sovereign, Not Man

For the LORD is our judge, the LORD is our lawgiver, the LORD is our king: He will save us (Isa. 33:22).

"The voice of a god and not of a man!" (Acts 12:22). Herod believed and acted on the words of his subjects. He fell for the delusion that those who rule are self-styled gods, independent of God's government over them. God did not take long to remind Herod and his worshipers that He alone rules in heaven and earth, and all rulers are subject to His sovereignty and law. Herod became a diet for worms: "And immediately an angel of the Lord struck him because he did not give God the glory, and he was eaten by worms and died" (12:23).

Today, the United States finds herself in the midst of making a similar choice. It's true that our coins have "In God We Trust" stamped on them. But it's probably equally true that our nation puts more trust in money than in God who supplies all wealth. Have we come to the place where we now believe that "My power and the strength of my hand made me this wealth" (Deut. 8:17)? God's assessment of such presumption is not easy for an unrepentant nation to take:

But you shall remember the LORD your God, for it is He who is giving you power to make wealth, that He may confirm His covenant which He swore to your fathers, as it is this day. And it shall come about if you ever forget the LORD your God, and go after other gods and serve them and worship them, I testify against you today that you shall surely perish. Like the nations that the LORD makes to perish before you, so you shall perish; because you would not listen to the voice of the LORD your God (Deut. 8:18–20).

These verses tell us why the first commandment must be our starting point for the proper ordering of ourselves, our families, our churches, and our nation. We must never put any of man's laws before the first commandment: "I am the LORD your God . . . you shall have no other gods before Me" (Ex. 20:2–3). Adherence to the first commandment protects us from those who would rewrite it to read "I, the State, am your God. You shall have no other gods before me." This is the first point in the biblical covenant structure: the absolute sovereignty of a transcendent God who is always present with His people. He sets up a hierarchy (point two), lays down the law (point three), judges men continually and also at the end of time (point four), and preserves His kingdom against all opposition (point five). When a ruler decrees either by word or deed that he is independent of God's government, or that justice is defined according to his self-made laws, or that man looks to the State for salvation, then God responds with judgment. A nation might not see God's judgment in the same way Herod did, but time brings all things to light. Choosing man as the sovereign ruler, independent of God, will lead a nation to slavery and eventual destruction.

God Speaks or Newspeak?

For the despotic ruler, power is all that matters. Words and what they mean, or what they are made to mean, are used to change opinions. When man makes up his own meaning on the basis of his own power, chaos results. Then a power struggle takes place among those who want their word to rule. For the humanist, power determines meaning.

What if a change in meaning results in the erosion of legitimate power and authority from individuals, families, churches, business establishments, and city, county, and state governments? What if "government of the people, by the people, and for the people" becomes "government over the people in the name of the people"? What if this change in definition works for the creation of a single political entity that sees itself as "God walking on earth"? What if the denial of God's many jurisdictional governments means that the State, a centralized civil government, becomes the all-embracing power that orders society through power, all in the name of security, peace, and prosperity?

In George Orwell's terrifying novel *1984*, "Newspeak" was the official language of "Oceania," a futuristic society where the ever-present Big Brother reigned supreme. "The purpose of Newspeak," Orwell writes, "was not only to provide a medium of expression for the world-view and mental habits proper to the devotees of Ingsoc [Newspeak for 'English Socialism'], but to make all other modes of thought impossible."[1]

The purpose in redefining words is to get people to think one-dimensionally, to think in terms of the newly formulated definition and no other. A purposeful shift in meaning has taken place with the word "government." Today, when the word government is used, an all-inclusive civil government is what most people have in mind, obliterating by definition the legitimate governments of family, church, and city, county, and state governments.

Noah Webster Speaks

The definition of "government" has changed over the years where now it has the exclusive meaning of the "the State," that is, civil government at the national level. Noah Webster's *An American Dictionary of the English Language,* first published in 1828, defined government broadly:

> GOVERNMENT, n. Direction; regulation. "These precepts
> will serve for the government of our conduct."

2. Control; restraint. "Men are apt to neglect the government of their temper and passions."

3. The exercise of authority; direction and restraint exercised over the actions of men in communities, societies or states; the administration of public affairs, according to the established constitution, laws and usages, or by arbitrary edict. "Prussia rose to importance under the government of Frederick II."

4. The exercise of authority by a parent or householder. "Children are often ruined by a neglect of government in parents. Let family government be like that of our heavenly Father, mild, gentle and affectionate."

All human government, as defined by Webster, begins with the individual in self-government or self-control (Gal. 6:23; Acts 24:25). Self-government undergirds all other types of governmental expression, including mothers and fathers in family government, elders and deacons in church government, and civil servants ("ministers") at all jurisdictional levels in civil government. For Webster, "government" means more than *civil* government.

Where did these early definers of government get these fundamental ideas? From the Bible. When the Bible speaks of "government" in the singular, it refers to the government of Jesus Christ that encompasses all of life including earthly governments:

For a child will be born to us, a son will be given to us; and the government will rest on His shoulders; and His name will be called Wonderful Counselor, Mighty God, Eternal Father, Prince of Peace. There will be no end to the increase of His government or of peace, on the throne of David and over His kingdom, to establish it and to uphold it with justice and righteousness from then on and forevermore. The zeal of the LORD of hosts will accomplish this (Isa. 9:6–7).

God's government is as comprehensive as His creation. He created all things; He rules over all things. Government in the singular—"His government"—belongs to Him alone. All earthly governments are temporal, limited in authority and jurisdiction, and prone to disruption and tyranny.

The One Government of God

The biblical concept of "government" has a comprehensive definition that includes self-government, family government, church government, and civil government. The operation of these plural governments is dependent upon the one government of God as expressed throughout the Bible. Jesus "upholds all things by the word of His power" (Heb. 1:3), and "for by Him all things were created, both in the heavens and on earth, visible and invisible, whether thrones or dominions or rulers or authorities—all things have been created by Him and for Him. And He is before all things, and in Him all things hold together" (Col. 1:16–17). Without God's government, there is no real legitimacy to earthly governments. The Declaration of Independence states, "We are endowed by our Creator with certain unalienable rights." The assumption is that without God there can be no rights. Since human governments are instituted to protect those rights, a point also made by the Declaration, it must also be assumed that human government is also a gift of God.

God is the model for all types of governments. The study of the law given by God to individuals, families, churches, and nations will show that these divine directives reflect God's character and His attributes. For example, the individual is to be holy as God is holy; the love that Jesus expressed in giving His life for the church is to be copied by husbands in their love for their wives (Eph. 5:22–34); the discipline that fathers give their children is a model of God's discipline of His children (Heb. 12:1–13); the State, as a civil governor, is God's "minister . . . an avenger who brings wrath upon the one who practices evil" (Rom. 13:4; cf. 12:19).

How does the principle of the "many" governments work itself out in family, church, and State? Children are commanded to obey their parents in the Lord (Eph. 6:1). There is real authority here and parents have jurisdiction within their own family structure as delegated and designed by God. God, not the State, defines the family.

Church members are part of a jurisdictional government called "ecclesiastical government." The church is given the "keys of the kingdom of heaven," and with these keys the leadership can "bind" and "loose" within the church (Matt. 16:19). The church, that is, those who are called as leaders (elders), have the jurisdictional authority to excommunicate unrepentant members (Matt. 18:15–18). The church is even given power to handle legal matters that many would see as the exclusive power of the State (1 Cor. 6:1–11). In the book of Hebrews, we are told to "Obey your leaders, and submit to them; for they keep watch over your souls, as those who will give an account" (Heb. 13:17). Ultimately, God will demand an accounting from us regarding our obedience to all levels of authority, including the civil magistrate.

The State has the power of the sword: "It does not bear the sword for nothing" (Rom. 13:4). Because the State has legitimate but delegated authority, Peter can write: "Submit yourselves for the Lord's sake to every human institution, whether to a king as the one in authority, or to governors as sent by him for the punishment of evildoers and the praise of those who do right" (1 Peter 2:13–14). Of course, the authority of the civil magistrate is limited in the same way that parents' authority over their children is limited and the church's authority over its members is also limited.

The One and the Many

God has established numerous authorities for the proper ordering of society. Mothers and fathers have authority over their children (Prov. 6:20–21; 15:5; 30:17; Eph. 6:1–3; Col. 3:20). Church leaders, elders and deacons, hold authority in the church (Matt.16:19; 18:15–20; 1 Thess. 5:12, 13; 1 Tim. 5:17–18; Heb. 13:17; 1 Peter 5:1–3). Civil rulers exercise political authority by God's decree (Matt. 22:21; Rom. 13:1–7; 1 Peter 2:13–14).

In other relationships, contracts can bind individuals and groups subject to the stipulations of a contract. The employer/employee relationship is contractual and carries with it legitimate authority (Lev. 19:13; Deut. 25:4; 1 Tim. 5:18; cf. Matt. 10:10; Luke 10:7). The courts, the judicial arm of civil authority, enforce the obligations of contracts by punishing the contract-breaker and seeing to it that restitution is paid to the contract-keeper. A contract is based on God's covenantal design. God sets forth obligations, benefits for obeying and reprisals for breaking covenant stipulations. Organizations can lawfully enforce contracts like God enforces His covenants.

The concept of multiple delegated authorities is patterned after the Divine One and Many—the triune nature of the Godhead. There is one God (Unity) and there are three Persons (Diversity) in the Godhead, each of whom is God. Each member of the Godhead—Father, Son, and Holy Spirit—has authority (unity of purpose in the exercise of authority), yet each performs a different task in history (diversity of function in the use of authority to accomplish the one purpose). The Triune God has impressed His creation with this divine pattern. Thus, He has ordained the family, the church, and civil governments as institutions, lesser authority structures, under His jurisdiction: many institutions but united by one purpose and duty—obedience to God for His glory.

Anarchy

The word anarchy is made up of two Greek words, *a* ("without") and *arche* ("rule" or "power"). An anarchist rejects any outside control or power of any of his personal actions. An anarchist feels justified in working in a violent way to overthrow any authority that works to curtail any of his individual freedoms, no matter how deviant or dangerous to the broader society.

Modern-day terrorism is a manifestation of anarchy under the guise of "freedom." There were those in 1960's counter culture who fostered anarchy as a way of reversing the order of society. Violent revolution was a synonym for reform. (See chapter 12). The revolutionary anarchist believes in the inherent goodness of some men, and that with an overthrow of the existing order and the death of the remaining evil men, a new society will emerge from the rubble.

Anarchy historically is the way of losers and short-sighted thinkers. It is not surprising to learn that when Lenin began to consolidate his power in Russia after the Russian Revolution, he deported the anarchists or had them shot. Yet they had supported revolutionary violence in the name of abolishing all political and State authority. There will always be State authority. The question is: Whose? God's authority or the authority of some petty dictator? The Bible's authority or the authority of the unbridled will of the people that led to the bloody French Revolution?

Autocracy

Another attempt at solving the dilemma of political power, either in the one or the many, is to consolidate it in one man, to create a messianic figure. An autocrat is someone who is an independent ruler. Absolute power (*kratos*) resides in the individual (*auto*=self). He continues in power by his own decree and is backed by military might. In the book of Judges we find the Israelites harassed by the Midianites: "And the power of Midian prevailed against Israel. Because of Midian the sons of Israel made for themselves the dens which were in the mountains and the caves and the strongholds" (Judges 6:2).

Israel's predicament was the result of disobedience: "Then the sons of Israel did what was evil in the sight of the LORD; and the LORD gave them into the hands of Midian seven years" (6:1). Instead of turning to God in repentance, the people looked for a *political* solution to their problems. The people were trusting in their man-made "tower" (8:9). Instead of putting their trust in God as their "Mighty Fortress" (Psalm 46), they chose the supposed power of man and man's temporary fortresses. Gideon promised to "tear down this fortress," the idol of security and salvation (8:9; cf. v. 17).

After Gideon defeated the enemies of Israel, the people were ready to set up a centralized political regime: "The men said, 'Rule over us, both you and your son, also your son's son, for you have delivered us from the hand of Midian'" (8:22). The problem the Israelites had with the Midianites occurred because they had rejected God as their King. Now that God had delivered them, they still failed to acknowledge that "The LORD should rule over them" (8:23). Instead, they opted for a centralized, humanistic, and perpetual social order with Gideon and his family as permanent rulers. To them, Gideon was more than a judge, a localized civil ruler, he was to be their king who would sit on a throne and make them secure. A centralized social order is better for man than putting one's trust for safety and security in the Lord and His decentralized governmental order!

With forty years of peace behind them, the people had forgotten who brought them peace (cf. Deut. 8). The people began to "play the harlot with the Baals, and made Baal-berith their god" (Judges 8:33). Once again, the rejection of God as their King led them to look to man and some sort of centralized social order. Abimelech attempted to centralize power and authority and place all sovereignty in himself. Abimelech took advantage of the weakened commitment of the people to the Lord. If they were ready to worship a synthetic god (Baal-berith means "Baal of the Covenant"—a mixture of Baalism and the promises of the biblical covenant), then they might have been ready to rally around him for security, a synthetic king. (Abimelech's father was an Israelite, while his mother was a Canaanite.) To ensure his scheme to power, Abimelech killed off all his political competition: "He went to his father's house at Ophrah, and killed his brothers the sons of Jerubbaal, seventy men, on one stone" (9:5).

Jotham escaped the bloodbath at Ophrah and went to Mount Gerizim to warn the Israelites not to rally around a king who promised security and at the same time demanded unconditional loyalty. The result of such an alliance would mean their destruction. Abimelech told them, "If in truth you are anointing me as king over you, come and take refuge in my shade [the promise of security]; but if not, may fire come out from the bramble and consume the cedars of Lebanon" (9:15). As with all centralized political regimes, judgment and ruin are inevitable. This centralized administration of Abimelech was made up of "worthless and reckless fellows" from Shechem (9:4). It was not long before the administration of this new dynastic ruler fell into ruin:

> God sent an evil spirit between Abimelech and the men of Shechem; and the men of Shechem dealt treacherously with Abimelech, in order that the violence done to the seventy sons of Jerubbaal might come, and their blood might be laid on Abimelech their brother, who killed them, and on the men of Shechem, who strengthened his hands to kill his brothers. And the men of Shechem set men in ambush against him on the tops of the mountains, and they robbed all who might pass by them along the road; and it was told to Abimelech (9:23–25).

An autocratic government is inherently unstable. Assassination and political coups are always a temptation for other ambitious men seeking the same power. The people are rarely safe or secure. Each successive ruler often changes the rules and regulations at his own whim. The people have little if any input into the workings of the government. There is no check on the king's power. Samuel Rutherford (1600–1661), in an attempt to counter the "divine right of kings" position, which was nothing more than autocratic government, wrote *Lex, Rex: or The Law and the Prince* (1644). Rutherford's position put even the king under God's Law. To no one's surprise, *Lex, Rex* was outlawed in England and Scotland.

Oligarchy

The word "oligarchy" is derived from a Greek word meaning "rule (*archein*) by the few (*oligos*)." In our day, the Supreme Court acts as an oligarchy. The justices on the Court are considered the final court of appeal. The law is what five of nine members say it is. The Court is a closed system. Nothing outside the Court, nothing higher than the

Court, rules. While Congress can overrule the Supreme Court, it rarely, if ever, happens.

What restrains the Court from overstepping its constitutional authority? As Supreme Justice Harlan Fiske Stone remarked in 1936, "While unconstitutional exercise of power by the executive or legislative branches of the Government is subject to judicial restraint, the only check upon our own exercise of power is our own sense of restraint."[2] But the very purpose of government is to check the unwillingness of man always to monitor his self-restraint. To give absolute control of government to a small group of men and women flies in the face of the biblical doctrine of total depravity.

Power in the hands of a few whose only check is their own "sense" of what they believe is right or wrong at any given moment in time puts a nation at risk. "Power corrupts," said Lord Acton, "and absolute power corrupts absolutely." What happens if the philosophy chosen by the court is assumed to be just and right and yet results in the tyranny of the masses? What happens when such a small group of judges pronounce that an unborn child is not protected by the Constitution, that he has no rights, that his "mother" has the constitutional right to kill him at will? Seven of nine justices, an oligarchy for life, sentenced 1.5 million unborn babies to death each year in America when they ruled in 1973 that abortion would be legal. On January 21, abortion was illegal; on January 22, abortion was legal. Seven of nine judges had spoken and made it so.

Democracy

Most Americans are under the false impression that our system of constitutional government is a democracy. To be sure, there are certainly democratic elements present. The First Amendment to the Constitution states, "The people" have the right "to petition the Government for a redress of grievances." The petition of the people is limited, however, by the procedures outlined in the Constitution to make those changes. Constitutional attorney John W. Whitehead writes: "It must be remembered that the term *democratic* appears neither in the Declaration of Independence nor in the Constitution. Actually, when the Constitution is analyzed in its original form, the document is found to be a serious attempt to establish a government mixed with democratic, aristocratic, and monarchical elements—a government of checks and balances."[3]

A democracy places all power in the people. It's a government of the masses. (The word "of" is tricky. It can mean "by" or it can mean "over." The bloody tyrannies of our day have been imposed *over* the people *in the name of* the people.) Democratic law is based on the will of the majority. In the *Federalist Papers*, which were popular newspaper articles written by Alexander Hamilton, James Madison, and John Jay in defense of the ratification of the Constitution, democracies were described as "spectacles of turbulence and contention,"said to be "incompatible with personal security or the rights of property. . . . In general [they] have been as short in their lives as they have been violent in their deaths."

Democracies degenerate into exploitation because rulers discover that if they promise certain benefits to a majority of voters, they can get those voters to put them in power. These voters realize that with their chosen ruler now in power, they can pressure him to vote in their best interests by threatening not to vote for him in the next election. The following quotation is attributed to Alexander Tytler[4] (1748–1813), Scottish professor of history at Edinburgh University and author of *The Decline and Fall of the Athenian Republic* (1776), and expresses the inherent dangers of a pure democracy:

> A democracy cannot exist as a permanent force of government. It can only exist until the voters discover that they can vote for themselves largesse [benefits] from the public treasury. From that moment on, the majority always votes for the candidate promising the most benefits from the public treasure, with the result that democracy always collapses over loose fiscal policy, always foiled by dictatorship.

Those seeking expression for heir views through majority rule will most often vote for the candidate promising the most benefits. The results are certain: Democracies eventually collapse because the public treasury is milked dry due to greater demands by the majority of voters. The minority of wage earners realize that no matter how hard they work, the fruit of their labor will be confiscated to satisfy the demands of the majority.

Socialism

Socialism, as a political and economic system, continues to attract adherents around the world. Socialism is not always practiced in the same way or with the same degree of centralized control. In the former Soviet Union, China, and Cuba, governmental control of the individual is nearly absolute. There is almost no freedom of movement. The former socialistic government of East Germany built a wall around the divided city to keep freedom-loving East Germans from fleeing to the freedom offered in the West. Under full-blown socialism, the State interferes in the everyday affairs of the people, even in the transactions they make. The State determines what will be produced, how much of it will be produced, how it will be produced, where it will be produced, by whom it will be produced, what price it will sell for, how people will get the product, and how it will be used. Under extreme forms of socialism, the individual is given little incentive to invent, produce a better product, or to be more efficient so a product can be sold at a lower price. The State determines everything. Incentive to invent is lost.

Milder forms of socialism allow for individual freedoms, but over time these freedoms are gradually taken away. Property rights are never absolute. The taxing power of the State increases in order to fund increased government programs always with the promise to create a better society. Socialists claim that it is the duty of the State to implement laws to break down economic and social "inequities," a form of class warfare, pitting the "rich" over against the "poor." While some socialists have had good intentions, the effect of socialist policies have been disastrous. Rich and poor do reach parity under a socialist system—everybody becomes poor.

One of the first attempts at a socialistic economy took place in colonial America at Jamestown (1607), hundreds of years before Karl Marx wrote the definitive work on socialistic economics, *Das Kapital*. For the first four years, all property was held in common. There were no individual property rights. The work was also communal. All of what was harvested was put in a single centralized storehouse. Since everybody got an equal share no matter how much work any individual performed, there was no incentive to work harder than the next person. Historians record that after four years, no crops were planted, houses were falling apart, and the main occupation of the men was bowling in the streets. The Jamestown Colony ultimately failed because the necessary incentives to work were taken away. Socialism begins with "interventionism," the gradual manipulation of the economy through governmental decree.

The history of the Plymouth Colony (1620) is a study in contrasts. Early attempts at a common storehouse similar to what was tried at Jamestown were quickly abandoned. Every member of the colony was given his own plot of land to cultivate as he pleased. In just one year, even after losing half their members to death, the Pilgrims of Plymouth were so prosperous, they were able to celebrate a bountiful thanksgiving feast. In 1621, Richard Winslow wrote from Plymouth back to England, stating: "I never in my life remember a more seasonable year than we have here enjoyed. We are so far from want that we often wish you partakers of our plenty. You might, on our behalf, give God thanks, who hath dealt so favorably with us."

Constitutional Republic

At the close of the Constitutional Convention, a woman supposedly asked Benjamin Franklin what type of government the Constitution established. The story goes that Franklin replied, "A republic, if you can keep it." Whether or not the story is true, Article IV, Section 4 of the U.S. Constitution includes the following directive: "The United States shall guarantee to every State in this Union a Republican Form of Government."

In a republican[5] form of government, authority is derived through the election of officials who serve as representatives of the people. These elected representatives are bound contractually by oath to uphold the principles outlined in the Constitution. They have a duty to protect the inherent rights of the citizenry. There is no divine right of kings or monarchical succession in a republican form of government. The attitude toward law is the administration of justice in accord with fixed moral principles and established evidence with a strict regard to consequences. A republican form of government avoids the dangerous extremes of either autocracy or pure democracy.

Many assume that since republicanism has worked well in America that it should have equal success elsewhere. The belief is that governmental *forms* are considered to be more important than worldviews and character. This has not proved to be true. Consider Bolivia. An attempt was made to govern this South American nation using our Constitution as a model. Simon Bolivar (1783–1830), who has been described as the "George Washington of South America," died an "exhausted and disillusioned idealist" because of the character of the ungovernable people.[6] He understood that self-government was as important as a proper governmental form. The people and elected officials must be willing to be governed by republican principles and follow fixed moral standards. Some months before his death Bolivar wrote:

> There is no good faith in [Latin] America, nor among the nations of [Latin] America. Treaties are scraps of paper; constitutions, printed matter; elections, battles; freedom, anarchy; and life a torment.[7]

A republican form of government is not perfect since imperfect people rule and are ruled. It is considered to be the best form of government because it takes into account the sinful nature of men and women by checking and balancing power and authority which has the effect of diminishing the threat that any one branch of government or the people generally will dominate the nation politically.

Summary Concepts

The first principle of government is that God is in charge. Human government must begin with *self-government under God*. Most people define government solely in political terms. But government is multi-faceted, covering numerous jurisdictions. Government in the singular belongs to God alone. God has established multiple governing authorities, one of which is *civil* government. These many authorities were not designed to compete but to cooperate. Multiple created authorities are patterned after the Divine One and Many, the Triune God. The One is not to be exalted over the Many. The Many are not to be exalted over the One. The many governments established by God are placed over a domain designated by God in Scripture. Civil government is God-ordained government and has a limited jurisdiction that is designed to punish evil doers and promote the good in civil affairs.

Summary Points

1. Rulers speak in the name of the god of the society.
2. Societies are therefore ruled either by the words of God or by the words of men.
3. A nation that forgets God is doomed in history.
4. God is the ultimate source of peace and prosperity.
5. To say that any human institution provides us with peace and prosperity is to make a god of that institution.
6. God judges institutions that rule in the name of any other god.
7. The words of man can be manipulated by men.
8. One source of political power in history has been the ability of rulers to redefine words.
9. A shift in meaning has taken place in the word "government" so that it only applies to the State.

10. Noah Webster's 1828 dictionary defined all government as beginning with self-government under God's government.
11. The Bible teaches that human governments are plural.
12. In the Bible, "the" government (singular) refers only to the rule of Christ.
13. God is the model for all governments.
14. God is Triune: both One and Many.
15. Anti-Christian views of government destroy either the unity or diversity of society.

Notes

1. George Orwell, *1984* (New York: Harcourt, Brace and Company, 1949), 303.

2. *United States v. Butler*, 297 U.S. 1 (1936); dissenting, 78.

3. John Whitehead, *The Separation Illusion* (Milford, Michigan: Mott Media, 1977), 47.

4. His named is often spelled "Tyler."

5. Not to be confused with the Republican Party in the same way that democratic is not to be confused with the Democrat Party.

6. Edward Coleson, "The American Revolution: Typical or Unique?," *The Journal of Christian Reconstruction*, Symposium on Christianity and the American Revolution, ed. Gary North, 3:1 (Vallecito, CA: Chalcedon, 1976), 176–77.

7. Quoted in Edward Coleson, "The American Revolution: Typical or Unique?," 177.

A Bottom-Up Hierarchy

Now listen to me: I shall give you counsel, and God be with you. You
will be the people's representative before God, and you bring the
disputes [of the people] to God, then teach them the statutes and the
laws, and make known to them the way in which they are to walk, and
the work they are to do. Furthermore, you shall select out of all the
people able men who fear God, men of truth, those who hate dishonest
gain; and you shall place these over them, as leaders of thousands, of
hundreds, of fifties and of tens. And let them judge the people at all
times; and let it be that every major dispute they will bring to you, but
every minor dispute they themselves will judge. So it will be easier for
you, and they will bear the burden with you (Ex. 18:19–23).

Moses faced a problem. Everyone seemed to be suing everyone
else, and they had only been out of Egypt for a month. Slaves cannot
govern themselves well, and the Isrealites were no exception. These recently freed slaves could not settle their own disputes, so they lined up
in front of Moses' tent daily in pursuit of justice.

Jethro, Moses' father-in-law, saw what was happening. He sug-
gested a solution. First, serve as God's representative, an intermediary
between God and the people. Second, teach them God's law, so they
will know what to do. In time, they will learn to govern themselves.

Third, establish an appeals court system, with righteous men serving as judges. Let these governors take the easier cases, saving the hard ones for you to take before God.

What was Jethro really saying? "You are not God; you need help. Acknowledge your weaknesses and limitations, share in the authority of being a judge, and you will not wear out these people, nor will they wear you out. In short, don't imitate Pharaoh who thought of himself as a god. Pharaoh's way is the way of destruction. Don't treat these people as slaves, even if they want to be slaves. God has delivered you out of Egypt; don't go back to Egypt governmentally."

Jethro recognized a basic fact of institutional life: the second point in the biblical covenant, that is, the necessity of hierarchy. There has to be a system of policy-making, and also a system of appeals. To what extent are policies set at the top and at the bottom? Where does primary institutional sovereignty lie, at the top or the bottom? The question facing Moses was this: Which kind of human hierarchical authority structure is required by God, top-down or bottom-up?

Egypt's Bureaucratic Theocracy

The Great Pyramid of Cheeps or Khufu, at Gizeh near Cairo, is the only surviving edifice of the Seven Wonders of the World. The Great Pyramid is a solid mass of limestone blocks, covering 13 acres. It contains about 2.3 million blocks that weigh an average of two and a half tons each. If laid end to end, they would stretch two-thirds of the way around the earth at the equator. In its original state it was 768 ft. square and 482 ft. high. The Great Pyramid and the smaller pyramids are a lasting testimony to the building prowess of the Egyptians. They are also evidence of the religion and political theory of Egypt. The very shape of the pyramids tells us something about Egypt's political philosophy. Egypt was a top-down system of total control. The Pharaohs believed in political centralization. All of life was controlled through the Pharaoh's decree. Who built the pyramids for the Pharaohs? The people, of course. Voluntarily? Certainly not. The pyramids were the classic public works program of all time: very expensive, but without any long-term benefits, except for rulers trying to make a name for themselves on both sides of the grave. The Pharaohs were not incorporating a new idea in the development of their political philosophy. All those who reject the true God want to be "like God" (Gen. 3:5). God is the controller of all things. Rebels against God want to control, to manipulate, and eventually to enslave. This is the dream of all empire-builders. Given enough power and authority, these power merchants believe that all of life can be controlled by man and for man.

Pyramid Power

The Tower of Babel, the first "Tower of Power," is a good place to start in our understanding of the nature of political power. These early empire-builders wanted to make a name for themselves (Gen. 11:4) by supplanting the government of God and replacing it with a centralized, bureaucratic system where all of life would be controlled from Babel. Making a name for themselves, like naming in general, is an act of *sovereignty* (Gen. 2:20, 23; Dan. 1:6–7).

In Genesis 11 we find the purposeful attempted overthrow of God's order and the elimination of God's name. Those involved in this conspiracy (see Psalm 2) were humanistic, man-centered kingdom-builders who wanted to consolidate their efforts and establish Babel as the political center.

The symbol of centralized power was the tower: "I will ascend to heaven; I will raise my throne *above* the stars of God, and I will sit on the *mount* of the assembly in the recesses of the north. I will *ascend* above the heights of the clouds; I will make myself like the Most High" (Isa. 14:13–14). God's government is the only centralized government. He is the Planner. The builders of the tower wanted to be what God is. The tower represented the seat of power—God's throne. Those who built the tower wanted to rise above "the stars of God" (Isa. 14:13). In Scripture, stars often represent rulers and/or kingdoms (Judges 5:20; Dan. 8:10; Matt. 24:29; Mark 13:25). According to Babylonian mythology, the gods made their throne and counseled together in the far north. In effect, the dictators in Babel wanted to rule the world. Their centralized kingdom would be located in the "land of Shinar." Power-hungry rulers, through the agency of civil government, would become like God as they ascended the Tower of Power, grabbing for more and more control over God's created order, centralizing power and subjugating the people to do their bidding.

Decentralization

In contrast to the pyramid system, God's system of political power is *decentralized*. No single institution has been established by God to bring about social order. Freedom and order are realized when men throughout a society strive to follow the blueprint God has given for the restoration and maintenance of all family, ecclesiastical, social, and political institutions. For example, Genesis 10 is a list of *many* families that represent a decentralized social order. The builders of Babel wanted to eliminate the *many* governments and consolidate family, ecclesiastical, and political power in the *one* State. God would have none of it. He "scattered them abroad from there over the face of the whole earth; and they stopped building the city" (Gen. 11:8).

All the kingdoms in Nebuchadnezzar's dream, an image of the Tower of Power, "were crushed all at the same time, and became like chaff from the summer threshing floors; and the wind carried them away so that not a trace of them was found" (Dan. 2:35). Man's Towers of Power will be "thrust down," "crushed," and "scattered." God's kingdom—God's government—will become "a great mountain" that will fill "the whole earth . . . and will itself endure forever" (2:35). While centralized political regimes will be "scattered," the government of Jesus Christ will have "no end" (Isa. 9:7).

Bearing in mind that God ordains authority, what should a biblical political structure look like? Should the pyramid and the tower be our examples? Should each individual be sovereign, every man doing what he believes is right in his own eyes (Judges 17:6)?

Government Under God

God has the ultimate authority to govern (Jer. 27:5; Prov. 8:15; 21:1; Matt. 28:18). If we were to make a diagram, it would be a hierarchy that looks something like this:

GOD
Independent and Unlimited Governing Authority
(Isaiah 9:6–7)

MAN AND HUMAN INSTITUTIONS
Dependent and Limited Governing Authority
(Exodus 18 and Romans 13:1–4)

Family	*Church*	*Civil (all levels)*
(Self-governing individuals under God)	(Self-governing individuals under God)	(Self-governing individuals under God)

Parents exercise authority over their children, employers over employees, teachers over students, elders or bishops over church members, and civil servants over citizens. In all these cases authority is backed up by penalties: a parent may discipline a child, an employer may fire an employee, a teacher may fail a student, the church may discipline or even excommunicate a member, and civil representatives may force a law-breaker to pay restitution for a crime.

The biblical pattern of authority establishes that God is the ultimate authority, and He alone establishes governments. In Romans 13:1 we are instructed to subject ourselves "to the governing authorities" because they are "established by God." Notice that there are *multiple* authorities. We owe no single earthly authority our total allegiance.

Those hostile to the Christian faith despise such biblically mandated governmental pluralism: a system that maintains there is one Law and one Lawgiver, but a plurality of jurisdictions or authorities to which all must submit. Such a system of government cannot be easily controlled. No one jurisdiction can claim the right to rule over all other established authorities. All are ultimately responsible to God for legitimacy. No authority can claim independence from the Triune God.

God's design in establishing multiple authorities means that no one government should cancel the authority of any other government. Ideally, all legitimate governments cooperate. They exist in the world by God's decree and design. Each exercises real power in its limited sphere of operation. The breakdown of authority comes when any authority abdicates legitimacy and responsibility and turns rulership over to a greater human authority hoping for security. In Old Testament Israel, family, church, and State were meant to operate under the jurisdiction of the One True King. As sin prevailed and judgment came, the people turned to the State for security. They abandoned personal, family, and ecclesiastical authority and responsibility and looked to the State for salvation. They rejected God as King over them and chose a king to judge them "like all the nations" (1 Sam. 8:5).

The people were looking for salvation. They were looking for someone to guarantee them their inheritance. God was rejected. The State became the god of the people.

Jurisdictional Diversity

When talking about authority and power as they relate to government, two extremes need to be avoided. The first extreme is the belief that the individual is a law unto himself, responsible only to himself. This extreme attempts to counter its opposite, that the *many* are ultimate. If the many were ultimate, anarchy would result. Many individuals could claim authority on their own terms.

Second, no one institution, group, nation, or society is ultimate. This opposes the idea that the one should be ultimate. If the one becomes ultimate, an institution, group, church, nation, or society can claim to be the final arbiter of truth and power, putting all diversity under its rule. Only God is ultimate; the one and the many are governed by God's Law in all things. Thus, the one and the many in society are balanced under the one authority of the Triune God.

Many delegated governments decentralize the centers of power. Corruption and tyranny are heightened when authority structures, from the individual to civil governments at the local, county, and state levels, break down, and all authority then rests in one institution, usually the State.

Reclamation of multiple authorities comes about when the individual assumes his responsibilities under God and thoroughly transforms his family, and working with other like-minded individuals, transforms his school, church, vocation, local community, state, and national civil government. We cannot expect diverse authority structures to rise on their own, however. Regeneration, the basis and beginning of all godly authority, begins with God working in the individual, and it extends to every facet of life.

Looking for Relief

A word of caution is needed here. Too often Christians turn to the State for relief because of the failure of individuals, families, businesses, schools, churches, and civil governments at the local, county, and state levels. The State has limited jurisdiction and competence, and is not man's answer for sin, except in temporal punishment for criminal acts. In fact, as recent history so well proves, the State frequently compounds the ills of society—the economy, education, welfare, the courts—when it acts outside of the area of its proper authority and jurisdiction.

It has been established that all authority belongs to God and that all earthly authority, whether family, church or State, is delegated and limited. The delegation of authority is purposely multiplied. This hampers the sinful tendency toward tyranny of any one governmental institution. For example, the authority of the State is not the same as that of a father who exercises authority as head of his household.

While each government should follow guidelines laid down in Scripture for its particular area of jurisdiction, not all biblical laws apply to each jurisdiction in the same way. Laws found in Scripture give parents the authority to exercise discipline over a child with a rod, but not over an erring brother in Christ. This authority belongs to the church. The church can discipline a member, but cannot use the rod or wield the sword as punishment. The church has the power of the "keys" to bar unrepentant members from the Lord's table and finally excommunicate them if they remain unrepentant (Matt.18:15–20).

The State has authority to wield the sword as punishment for capital offenses (Rom. 13:4), but it cannot use its authority to influence the inner workings of the family or church. These "governments" are outside its jurisdiction unless a crime is committed.

Jesus' words in Luke 20:22–25 establish the authority of the State and also set the boundaries for its civil jurisdiction. Men asked Him, "'Is it lawful for us to pay taxes to Caesar, or not?' But He detected their trickery and said to them, 'Show me a denarius. Whose head and inscription does it have?' And they said, 'Caesar's.' And He said to them, 'Then render to Caesar the things that are Caesar's, and to God the things that are God's.'" Jesus was not saying that God and Caesar are equal, for even Caesar is under God's authority (Rom. 13:1–4). We should also bear in mind that we do not live under Caesar today. We live under a written Constitution.

When the church disciplines a local church member over doctrinal matters, the State should not be approached to use its authority to override what the disciplined member might consider to be an unjust decision. Even the jurisdictional boundaries of ecclesiastical bodies must be respected, though this is difficult in a multi-denominational context. When one church disciplines a member and excommunicates that member, it is the duty of other ecclesiastical bodies to grant at least initial respect to the jurisdiction of the disciplining ecclesiastical court. This might include contacting the prospective member's home church to determine why the member left.

Jurisdictional authority can only be understood when the biblical "chain of authority" is considered. This follows under the theology of "headship." Paul writes, "But I want you to understand that Christ is the head of every man, and the man is the head of a woman, and God is the head of Christ" (1 Cor. 11:3). In Ephesians 5:23, Jesus is said to be the "head of the church" and "the ruler of the kings of the earth" (Rev. 1:5; Psalm 72). In all these cases we find everyone responsible to someone else, and ultimately all are responsible to God. Even Jesus in His humanity, as the Son of God, is under the headship of His Father (Luke 22:42).

The Biblical Answer: A Constitutional Republic

We find in Exodus 18 a description of what a decentralized civil government should look like. Moses, as God's unique representative, appointed righteous judges over the people in a hierarchy of authority. But this hierarchy was not a top-down pyramid. Rather, it was a bottom-up *appeals court*. God had given them His law (as He has given it to us), and the people were to take their disputes to God-fearing men who would render honest judgment. If a case was too hard for them, then the judges would refer it to the next level upward.

This leaves individuals free to work out their own salvation with fear and trembling (Phil. 2:12). Each person is to be self-governed under God. In ancient Israel, God required His law to be read to the whole nation every seventh year (Deut. 31:10–13) which revealed the terms of civil righteousness to everyone. Each person was made responsible for his actions. This is God's system of self-government. Only when people disagree about the legal boundaries between them do they call in the judges. Thus, there is liberty at the individual level, but there is also a court system for achieving peaceful settlements of disputes. This is the same sort of appeals system that Christ established for the settling of disputes in the church (Matt.18:15–20).

God therefore provided a hierarchy for them, but a bottom-up hierarchy. He gave them His law (Ex. 18:20). He made righteousness the fundamental principle of holding office: "Moreover you shall select from all the people able men, such as fear God, men of truth, hating covetousness; and place such over them as to be rulers of thousands, rulers of hundreds, rulers of fifties, and rulers of tens" (18:21).

The principle of biblical representative government stems from this Old Testament innovation. The primary issue is ethics—righteousness. Secondary to this is competence, but always secondary: Paul said that it is better to be judged by the least competent person in the church than by an anti-Christian civil judge (1 Cor. 6:4). Even so, Christians should strive for the highest levels of competence, wisdom, and character.

The representative is under God and sworn to uphold God's law. He represents men before God and God before men. All authority is God-given. God grants original authority to the ruled to choose who will rule over them. He therefore also grants authority to the rulers. Ultimately, if people refuse to obey rulers, they can topple any system of government. The people are sovereign, but they are not *originally* sovereign. Only God possesses original sovereignty.

Summary Concepts

The second basic principle in the Biblical blueprint for government is that God has established a hierarchical yet decentralized political order where neither the individual nor the group is ultimately sovereign. There are checks and balances in order to preserve liberty, authority, and stability. No single human institution or branch of civil government is absolutely sovereign. Only God is absolutely sovereign.

Authority and power to govern are delegated by God. Thus, those who govern are obligated to govern according to God's law, for they are ministers of God (Rom. 13:1–7). There really is no other option.

As a nation moves away from God as Governor of all of life, the State claims for itself more and more power. All competing governments are removed—usually by force, always by intimidation. In time, the people suffer under the weight of unbridled oppression. What was once a promise of security by those centralizing authority and power, becomes a choking tyranny. The oppression continues and turns the people either into slaves or rebels. The solution to the plight of tyranny is not to place authority and power in the hands of the individual. Nor is the solution found in the ruling abilities of a self-appointed elite.

Political centralization has been the prevailing trend in the history of the world. Egypt used the people to construct a society, using the energies of the masses to implement the goals of the State, governed by the Pharaohs. The pyramid, the tower, and Nebuchadnezzar's colossus are visible manifestations of centralized political planning. God calls for decentralized civil governments. His blueprint for life is decentralization, with the individual working and having freedom in the family, church, business, and civil government. No one man or institution is to rule over all other aspects of society. The way to a just order is not found in anarchy where man is a law unto himself, in socialism where the State owns the means of production, in an oligarchy where a planning elite rules and overrules, or in a democracy where the people can change the direction of a nation by whim and fancy. God has established a decentralized society best described as a Constitutional Republic where the best are elected to office and yet are still responsible to the vote of the people.

Summary Points

1. Slaves do not govern themselves well.
2. The civil government is an intermediary between God and man.
3. The civil government is to announce the laws of God.
4. The ruler is to appoint righteous judges to handle the less difficult cases.
5. This means that God wants men to establish governmental hierarchies (point two of the biblical covenant).
6. Egypt's hierarchy was bureaucratic: top down.
7. This was reflected in the design of the pyramids.
8. The Tower of Babel was another pyramid of power.
9. Only God centralizes power.
10. Decentralization is what God requires for man's governments.
11. God scattered those who built the Tower of Babel.
12. Man's governments (plural) are always hierarchical.

13. The Bible teaches pluralism: plural governments under God's unified law.

14. Governments possess multiple jurisdictions.

15. Too often Christians turn to the State for answers.

16. The Biblical solution for civil government is a constitutional republic.

17. This involves representative government.

18. Rulers are supposed to represent men to God and God to men.

19. Such authority is delegated originally to specific men from God, and secondarily from the ruled (who also possess God-given authority) to the rulers.

Plural Law Systems,
Plural Gods

---

*To the law and to the testimony! If they do not speak according to this
word, it is because there is no light in them (Isa. 8:20).*

Justice! What a long quest it has been for mankind. In every society,
men seek justice, and they never seem to find it. Why not? Because they
do not seek the God of the Bible, in whom alone there is perfect justice.
Why not? Because He dispenses perfect justice, and imperfect men know
what this means: "For all have sinned and fall short of the glory of God"
(Rom. 3:23). What men say they are seeking is honest judgment. But
honest judgment implies a standard: honest law. Honest judgment is
not based on the wishes of the few or the will of the mighty. It is based
on the wishes of the Mighty One. Honest judgment can only be secured when we turn to a law that rests outside the partisan interests of
fallen men. *Honest judgment must rest on objective norms of law and justice.* But modern man does not want to admit that such objective standards exist. He tells us to search elsewhere. Should we appeal to the
latest polling statistics? Is the United States Supreme Court the final
court of appeal for Americans?

The Bible says that the final court of appeal is the judgment seat of God: "Shall not the Judge of all the earth do justly?" (Gen. 18:25). There is unquestionably a Supreme Court, but it is not some national Supreme Court; it is a heavenly court. No earthly court of appeals should be given absolute and final jurisdiction.

Biblical Laws or Anti-Biblical Laws

The study of any subject must be placed within the limits of a biblical worldview. The third principle of the Biblical covenant is that God lays down the law to man. Man is supposed to exercise dominion by means of biblical law. To speak of justice, or anything else for that matter, as isolated from a biblical covenantal structure, is to lead us into a sea of ethical subjectivity. A recent example of such a quest for Bible-less law is the revival in some Christian and conservative political circles of a "natural law ethic" as a substitute for biblical law. (Humanist legal scholars do not take this revival seriously since they fully understand that Darwinian evolutionary thought destroyed any concept of humanistic natural law. Man makes his own rules in today's post-Darwin world.)

There is no neutrality in making laws. A law says one thing is right or wrong. This inevitably infringes on someone's money, lifestyle, or dreams. Who wins, who loses? If humanist man has his way, God will lose, as will all those who stand with God. When autonomous man's law prevails, we can expect God's law to be invalidated (Mark 7:8, 13).

Satan attacked God on the basis of His law: "Indeed, has God said, 'You shall not eat from any tree of the garden?'" (Gen. 3:1). He appealed to Adam and Eve to be a law unto themselves—to "be like God" (3:5). Even the devil knew there was no neutrality.

The appeal today is to ethical pluralism, everyone doing what is right in his own eyes (Judges 17:6). The God of Scripture has spoken, but so has the god of convenience, the god of tolerance, the god of expediency, the god of majority opinion, the god of experience, and the god of any other ethical system that seeks to be a part of America's legal mainstream.

One Lawgiver, One Law

In biblical terms, there is but one law and one Lawgiver. God thought enough of His law to send His Son to keep it in every detail. If the Son of God was required to keep the law, should anything less be expected of the sons of God? Jesus was tempted at every point with respect to obeying the commands of God, yet He remained sinless throughout His life (Heb. 4:15). He kept the law perfectly. There was no need for Jesus to offer up sacrifices for His own sins because He committed no sins (7:26–28). Instead, He offered Himself up as a lamb without blemish as the law required, in order to cleanse us of our sins (9:14).

The entire human race has been found "guilty" according to God's law. While the law ceases to condemn the Christian in terms of final judgment (Gal. 3:13), because of Jesus' perfect obedience and His substitutionary atonement, all people are held accountable to keep the law as a standard of right and wrong this side of heaven (Rom. 3:31). In the movie *O Brother, Where Art Thou?*, Everrett, played by George Clooney, reminds Delmar and Pete that while they are redeemed in the sight of God, they still owe a debt to the state of Mississippi for their criminal actions.

When a dispute arose among the people, Moses directed them to the law of God: "When they have a dispute, it comes to me, and I judge between a man and his neighbor, and make known the statutes of God and His laws" (Ex. 18:16). The judges appointed by Moses to share in the task of settling disputes also were required to judge according to the law of God (18:19–20). The people as a whole must be careful not to add to the law of God or take away from it (Deut. 4:2). This indicates that God's law must be used as it is and not mixed with the changing laws of men. Men often are tempted to adapt God's commandments to fit the times. Thus the judgment of man is deemed superior to that of God, and the commandments of God often are nullified.

The Levitical priests as well as the judges of Israel were required to follow the law. The people of Israel also were instructed to heed the judges' verdict because the decision was based upon the unchanging law of God and not upon the decision of men: "According to the terms of the law which they teach you, and according to the verdict which they tell you, you shall do; you shall not turn aside from the word which they declare to you, to the right or the left" (Deut. 17:11).

Reforming Society

When Jehoshaphat initiated reforms, one of the first areas of reformation was the judicial system: "And he appointed judges in the land in all the fortified cities of Judah, city by city. And he said to the judges, 'Consider what you are doing, for you do not judge for man but for the LORD who is with you when you render judgment. Now then let the fear of the LORD be upon you; be very careful what you do, for the LORD our God will have no part in unrighteousness, or partiality, or the taking of a bribe'" (2 Chron. 19:5–7). Reformation came from the top and the bottom. The decision of the judges must not issue from political or economic pressures or calculations, or any merely human purposes, but from obedience to the Lord of heaven, earth, and history, and to the righteous laws He has revealed to us in Scripture.

The prophets of Israel continued to warn the nation that only the law of God serves as a legal system's foundation: "To the law and to the testimony! If they do not speak according to this word, it is because they have no dawn" (Isa. 8:20). Any attempt to repudiate the law of God as a standard for righteousness establishes man as judge, lawgiver, king, and savior and has the effect of leaving man under the rule of darkness. The Bible clearly shows that law originates in the character of God, and definitions for justice and righteousness find their meaning in Him and not in the finite, fallible, and fallen nature of the creature: "For the LORD is our judge, the LORD is our lawgiver, the LORD is our king; He will save us" (Isa. 33:22):

- "The works of His hands are truth and justice; all His precepts are sure. They are upheld forever and ever; they are performed in truth and righteousness" (Psalm 111:7–8).
- "Thy testimonies are fully confirmed; holiness befits Thy

house, O LORD, forevermore" (Psalm 93:5).

- "All commandments are truth. Of old I have known from Thy testimonies, that Thou has founded them forever" (Psalm 119:151b–152).
- "The sum of Thy word is truth, and every one of Thy righteous ordinances is everlasting" (119:160).
- "The word of our God stands forever" (Isa. 40:8).

On the other hand, the word of man is feeble because his nature is finite and fallen: "All flesh is grass, and all its loveliness is like the flower of the field. The grass withers, the flower fades, when the breath of the LORD blows upon it; surely the people are grass. The grass withers, the flower fades, but the word of our God stands forever" (Isa. 40:6–8).

A Law Unto Themselves

The modern use of law is arbitrary, based in one case on a judge, in another, on the word of a Führer like Adolf Hitler. Thus man becomes the lawmaker, and the word of human authority becomes the new law. The courts, therefore, no longer are bound by any law. They have in effect become a law unto themselves.

As soon as Adam and Eve sinned, the accusations began. God cross-examined Adam and Eve, beginning with the responsible agent in the family, Adam. Adam blamed his wife, and ultimately God: "The woman whom Thou gavest to be with me, she gave me from the tree, and I ate" (Gen. 3:11). God then cross-examined Eve. Eve blamed the serpent: "The serpent deceived me, and I ate" (3:13). In other words, both of them blamed their environment. Both of them implicitly blamed the One who made their environment, God. But God was not responsible; neither was their environment. They lived in a paradise not a desert! Adam sinned wilfully, and was fully responsible. Eve sinned because she had been deceived (1 Tim. 2:14), but she was also fully responsible. God punished both of them for their sin (Gen. 3:16–19). He also punished the serpent (3:14), a punishment that promised ultimate victory to the seed of the woman over the forces of evil (3:15).

Murder (4:8, 23) and other acts of violence (6:2) then became part of the cursed created order. God therefore implemented laws to deal with the violence that resulted from man's sinful desires: "Whoever sheds man's blood, by man his blood shall be shed, for in the image of God He made man" (9:6). Laws protecting life (Ex. 20:15), property (20:13), and personal/neighbor relationships (20:12, 14, 16) were made part of the system of laws that Israel was bound to follow. Justice, therefore, was defined in terms of the law, God's law.

The Power of the Sword

Israel's governmental systems were decentralized. Judges and their officers, and the elders of the people were appointed to a variety of cities on the local level. They were responsible for administering justice in the locale where they were installed to power: "If a slain person is found lying in the open country in the land which the LORD your God gives you to possess, and it is not known who has struck him, then your elders and your judges shall go out and measure the distance to the cities which are around the slain one" (Deut. 21:1–2). Atonement had to be made for the death of a person found in an open field outside the boundaries of any particular city. The city closest to the slain body was responsible to make atonement. The city was represented by elders (representing civil affairs) and judges (representing judicial matters). While cities had numerous elders and judges, the law of God bound them to follow the same legal procedures. The law of God insured that people were being judged by "righteous judgment," no matter which judge kept court.

When a foundation of law is denied, those who rule in our nation's courts establish themselves and their own ethical "ideals" as the standards for righteousness. Often an individual who dislikes the verdict handed down in one court appeals to a higher court to find a judge who operates with a different set of judicial principles based upon a different law. Judicial decisions from state to state often differ because of the absence of any standard of righteousness.

In many courts throughout our land there is a decided bias *against* the Christian religion. Law has become sociological, pragmatic, and utilitarian. Law becomes a shifting foundation, determined by minorities that can whip up majorities to control the courts. Law loses its reliability. People then lose faith in the court system. The result is lawlessness, rebellion, and even greater efforts to centralize civil power.

Judicial Safeguards

The standard for justice already has been established by the Word of God. Judges are unable to judge rightly unless there is an appeal to some fixed moral standard. To operate contrary to justice is to deny the Word of God:

First, the status of a person involved in or accused of a crime would not be taken into account when he is judged. Fallen man tends to favor the rich because they hold greater influence in the community where the judge resides. The poor are easily disadvantaged because their meager living does not afford the options often available to the affluent. On the other hand, the poor often are pitied by social activists when they commit a crime, and thus are able to use their economic condition to arouse sympathy and to overrule requirements of the law. God's law makes no provision for favoring the rich or pitying the poor when a crime is committed: "You shall do no injustice in judgment; you shall not be partial to the poor nor defer to the great, but you are to judge your neighbor fairly" (Lev. 19:15).

Second, Paul says the "love of money is a root of all sorts of evil" (1 Tim. 6:10). The Bible warns the judge not to be influenced by bribes. Moreover, in choosing men for the office of judge, one requirement is that they "hate dishonest gain" (Ex. 18:21). Instead of seeing the law as the standard of judgment, money too often becomes the dispenser of justice to those who have money.

Third, the law of God is not one law among many to be chosen at will to fit only certain circumstances. The Asherah was a female deity of the Canaanites (Baal was the male counterpart) usually represented by a wooden pole or a luxuriant tree that was considered to be sacred. When the Israelites entered the land they were commanded to destroy the foreign sanctuaries so the pagan religion of the Canaanites would be rejected in the minds of the people. Any attempt to mix the prevailing religion of the day with the purity of the faith delivered to Israel was prohibited.

When a nation's judicial system seeks to institute a law system that mixes the law of God with the arbitrary laws of men, over a period of time God's law will be repudiated. The shift from a legal system based upon the law of God to a legal system based upon the wavering laws of men takes time, however. The shift is often imperceptible. *When man's laws, based upon the independent reasoning of the creature, are made equal with revelation, we can be assured that the new law system is in place.* Christians must know that there can be no so-called neutral system of law. When the law of God is replaced by any other system of law, that pagan system of law is an Asherah next to the altar of God.

Natural Law: A Wolf in Sheep's Clothing

There were many in the latter part of the eighteenth century who attempted to overthrow the Christian foundation of law by establishing the people's "collective conscience" (the so-called Social Contract) as the standard for law. Liberal John Locke and radical Jean Jacques Rousseau are the two most famous eighteenth-century Social Contract theorists. Natural law theory led to the establishment of an elite law-making group that determined the nature and direction the courts would take.

Darwinian evolution served as the death knell to the concept of absolute law. Law no longer was rooted in the Creator, but found its meaning in experience or in the evolving "natural order" of things. Autonomous reason has been erected in the courts of our day. The will of some earthly court is final. While the judicial system of the United States was originally established to interpret the Constitution in light of biblical law, along the lines laid down by William Blackstone, the court system now has set itself *above* the law where it *makes* law independent of any fixed authority.

It is unfortunate that in our day, when the world is crying for reliable and absolute standards to help in decision-making, many Christian scholars and leaders still appeal to a natural law solution, even though they know full well that its origins are suspect. According to Connaught Marshner, here is what passes for a "good system of ethics":

> Natural law ethics are adequate to the task. The philosophy
> of natural law has been time honored since the ancient Greeks.
> Though intellectual fashions change, the objective moral order,
> known by man and within the reach of mankind, can be reason-
> able seen as the most stable basis of personal, national and inter-
> national order and happiness.[1]

Marshner admits that natural law theory comes from ancient Greece, where the philosophies of Plato and Aristotle placed man at the center of the universe. She goes on to to say that these laws are "knowable by man" and "can be reasonably seen." Why then is there so much disagreement around the world as to what constitutes a just society if reason is the only problem? "Right Reason" certainly does not work in the minds of the Soviet leadership or in the mind of a pro-abortionist. The murder of nearly 100 million under atheistic communism, and the death of nearly 1.5 million unborn babies every year in the United States since 1973 are the result of the repudiation of biblical law in favor of an ever-evolving law. Whatever is at the moment, is right.

Those Christians who maintain that they have found a solution in natural law see it as equal to biblical law but without the religious trappings. We are told that we need "both" standards: biblical law for Christians and natural law for everyone else. Marshner continues:

> If order is to be restored to society, and the underpinnings
> of freedom preserved, America must return to non-consequen-

tial ethics. What would be the basis for such ethics? Some say the sole possible basis is revealed religion. *This is a mistake. First of all, the Bible and other revealed documents do not answer explicitly all the ethical questions that arise. . . .*[2]

If revealed religion (the Bible) is not the "sole possible basis" for decision-making, then what is? The Bible says "no one can serve two masters" (Matt.6:24). The apostle Paul writes that Christians are not to be unequally yoked with unbelievers (2 Cor. 6:14). How then can Christians be unequally yoked with unbelieving ethical systems? "For what partnership have righteousness and lawlessness, or what fellowship has light with darkness? Or what harmony has Christ with Belial, or what has a believer in common with an unbeliever?" (2 Cor. 14–15)

The premise of these natural law advocates is that the Bible cannot be used as an ethical handbook to deal with issues like "genetic screening, nuclear weapons systems, or in vitro fertilization" because "the scriptures speak only by interpretation."[3] But can't the same thing be said about every ethical system? There's always interpretation. Constitutional scholars admit that the Constitution declares that it is "the law of the land," but they often disagree on what it means and how its principles should be applied. At least with the Bible, we know that our starting point is reliable.

Natural law is flawed from its inception because it assumes that "nature" (a humanist substitute for the more accurate "creation") is not fallen, that man's reasoning abilities are not distorted due to the Fall, and that ethics is based on "philosophy" and not "religious precepts." Again, Mrs. Marshner has little use for the Bible in the legal process: "Citizens must defend their rights, and they must defend them intellectually, by employing and invoking an objective system of right and wrong. This new traditional system of ethics is based on *philosophical precepts, not on religious precepts, and can be understood and accepted by anyone willing to master the 'intellectual rigors of it.'*"[4] Who will determine what an "objective system of right and wrong" will be? What if the precepts of the Bible are rejected by those "willing to master the intellectual rigors" of these "philosophical precepts"? If history is any indicator, the Bible will be rejected in favor of self-serving, humanistic natural law that can be shaped and formed like wet clay. Religion is an enemy to natural law. Josef Stalin's words should silence all who appeal to the supposed inherent reasonableness of natural law: "We guarantee the right of every citizen to combat by argument, propaganda and agitation, any and all religion. The Communist Party cannot be neutral toward religion. It stands for science, and all religion is opposed to science."[5] So much for objectivity, "non-consequential ethics," and "philosophical precepts."

One last nail needs to be driven into the coffin of natural law. If natural law is adequate as a basis for ethical standards, why were the Israelites required to hear the revealed law read at least once every seven years? Gary North writes:

> Human reason, unaided by God's revelation untwisted by God's grace—cannot be expected to devise a universal law code based on any presumed universal human logic. What mankind's universal reason can be expected to do is to rebel against God and His law. Ethical rebels are not logically faithful to God.

Biblical law had to be read to everyone in Israel at least once every seven years (Deut. 31:10–13). God presumed that men would not understand His law unless they heard it (Deut. 31:13). Every resident of the land had to listen to this law. If the whole of biblical law had been ingrained into the consciences of all men from the beginning of time, or if the terms of the law, including the law's explicit penalties, were always available to all men through the exercise of man's universal reason, then the law would not have required the priests to read the Mosaic law before the congregation of Israel every seventh year.[6]

"The heart is deceitful above all things, and desperately wicked; who can know it?" (Jer. 17:9). That question of the prophet Jeremiah rings just as true today. The heart that says it can interpret neutral, universal, reasonable natural law is deceitful and desperately wicked. Who therefore can know natural law?

What is needed is an interpreter. The Bible is that interpreter. Many people may interpret the Bible differently, but over time, God rewards those who interpret it correctly and also apply it faithfully. God blesses those who are covenantally faithful. Thus, history progressively reveals true law from false law, though not without historical defeats of the faithful in periods of general apostasy (principle five of the covenant: continuity).

Summary Concepts

The third basic principle in the Biblical blueprint for civil government is that *God's law as revealed in the Bible is the standard for personal righteousness and national obedience.*

The world is looking for answers to life's most basic ethical problems. The promise of freedom under the lie of moral relativism has led our nation down the path of destruction and hopelessness. In our attempt to play god, we have turned into the worst kind of devils. We have fooled ourselves into believing that life without law is the closest thing to utopia. The definition of utopia, "no place," is the direction we're headed if we do not get back on the path God has set before us.

To what will we return? Will Christians lead the way with an objective, transcendent, and revealed law, or will we compromise with some brand of "natural law"? Now is the time for Christians to set forth the sure and clear Word of God to a world literally dying in a sea of moral subjectivism.

This is not the time for compromise. The saving work of Jesus Christ to redeem sinners dead in trespasses and sins and His law as a system of personal and societal righteousness are the only hope. If we opt for some morally neutral ethical system, then we will confront a world without Christ. Only the law of God is a tutor that will lead people to Christ. No other law system can do the job that God's law was designed to do.

A nation's judicial system rests on law—the law of God or the law of man. Both Church and State are bound to follow the law of God as revealed in Scripture. The modern understanding of law makes it arbitrary, and man becomes the standard for all ethical decision-making.

The State has the power of the sword to punish law breakers as defined by the Bible. Without God's law as the standard, the State is free to establish its own law. Public policy prevails. Politics is king. The individual must bow in submission to the will of the State.

The status of an individual involved in or accused of a crime is not to be taken into account when a judge hears his case. The Bible warns judges not to be influenced by money. The Law of God is not just one law among many. The acceptance of God's law is not an option for us as individuals or as a nation.

Natural law is inadequate as a standard for righteousness. Natural law is determined by man and man alone. The survival of the fittest is "natural." Should we enact such a principle into law? In effect, we have. The right of a woman to abort her defenseless unborn baby is the net result of a consistent natural law ethic.

Summary Points

1. Men have always sought justice.
2. God is the only true source of justice.
3. Honest judgment always rests on objective law.
4. The Bible tells men what a just legal system looks like.
5. Dominion is always exercised in terms of a specific view of the world.
6. To search for justice apart from the Bible is to pursue ethical subjectivism: many opinions, many voices, many laws.
7. Natural law is one such fruitless, self-defeating search.
8. Legal pluralism is the reign of subjectivism and relativism.
9. There is only one lawgiver, and therefore only one true law.
10. All people are held accountable before God to obey biblical law.
11. Jesus Christ met this legal standard perfectly.

12. Biblical reformation comes from both the top and the bottom: from rulers and ruled.
13. Modern law is arbitrary.
14. God judged Adam and Eve in terms of His law, not theirs.
15. The State possesses the power of the sword: violence.
16. Law is never neutral.
17. Modern laws are increasingly anti-Christian.
18. God has established safeguards for His law.
19. These safeguards are reduced when men mix rival views of law with biblical law.
20. Natural law is one such rival law system.
21. Who will establish which law is truly "natural"?
22. In the Old Testament, Biblical law had to be read to the people every seventh year; "natural law" was not sufficient.
23. God blesses covenantally faithful societies over time.
24. True law is thereby distinguished from rival laws.

Notes

1. Connaught Marshner, "Right and Wrong and America's Survival," *Future 21: Decisions for Amenia in the 21st Century* (Greenwich, CT: Devin-Adair, 1984), 129. Emphasis added.

2. Marshner, "Right and Wrong and America's Survival," 128. Emphasis added.

3. Marshner, "Right and Wrong and America's Survival," 128.

4. Marshner, "Right and Wrong and America's Survival," 132. Emphasis added.

5. "Declaration to American Labor Delegation," Moscow, September 7, 1927.

6. Gary North, *Moses and Pharaoh: Dominion Religion Versus Power Religion* (Tyler, Texas: Institute for Christian Economics, 1985), 236.

God Judges the Nations

And the LORD said, "The outcry of Sodom and Gomorrah is indeed great, and their sin is exceedingly grave. I will go down now, and see if they have done entirely according to its outcry, which has come to Me; and if not, I will know" (Gen. 18:20–21).

The day of doom was about to arrive for Sodom and Gomorrah. They had been the most blessed cities of the land of Canaan. It was to Sodom that Lot turned when Abraham offered him any place in the land. "And Lot lifted up his eyes and saw all the valley of the Jordan, that it was well watered everywhere this was before the LORD destroyed Sodom and Gomorrah like the garden of the LORD, like the land of Egypt as you go to Zoar" (Gen. 13:10).

God is the Judge of the nations. Judgment is the fourth point of the Biblical covenant structure. He created the earth. He also brought the judgment of the great flood. After the flood, God created the nations in an act of His sovereign judgment (Gen.10). After they attempted to create a one-world State (meaning a one-State world), He divided mankind linguistically at the Tower of Babel (11:1–9). The pyramid of power that mankind was about to build at Babel was destroyed by God.

He then scattered mankind across the face of the earth. This was a curse on mankind, yet it was also a blessing, for it withdrew men from the jurisdiction of a one-world bureaucratic State. It divided mankind into independent, sovereign, language-based nations, thereby destroying forever the possibility of fulfilling covenant-breaking man's dream of becoming a unified god. It decentralized political power, leaving men free to work out their cultural gifts and skills.

God went to Sodom and Gomorrah as a Judge. He went to see whether the sinful outcry of these cities was as bad as it sounded. Like Abel's blood crying to God from the ground (Gen. 4:10), sin cries up to God, and God hears. But as a Judge, He first conducts a trial, like the one He conducted in the garden, when He cross-examined Adam and Eve before bringing judgment, or just as He cross-examined Cain after Cain had murdered Abel. He gathers evidence. Then He judges it in the light of His law and finally announces His judgment and brings either blessings or cursings.

Collective Responsibility

Abraham bargained with God to spare Sodom (and therefore Lot) as soon as he was told that God was about to judge Sodom. "Wilt Thou indeed sweep away the righteous with the wicked?" Abraham asked (Gen. 18:23). Are righteous men who happen to be dwelling among the unrighteous also to be destroyed, just because of the sins of the immoral majority? God's answer was clear: *Yes.* Abraham knew this. But he haggled with God over the "price." "Will you spare the city for fifty righteous people?" Abraham's language is highly significant: "Far be it from Thee to do such a thing, to slay the righteous with the wicked, so that the righteous and the wicked are treated alike. Far be it from Thee! Shall not *the Judge of all the earth* deal justly?" (18:25). God is the Judge of "all the earth" and not just of some people at certain times in history. All nations are subject to His rule. His law is for *all the nations.*

God, knowing full well that there was but one righteous man in the city, was willing to promise Abraham that He would indeed spare the city for the sake of fifty righteous people. So Abraham tried to get a better deal. What about forty-five righteous people? God agreed: He would spare it for forty-five (18:28). And so it went, until Abraham got God to agree to spare the city for as few as ten righteous people (18:32).

Then God sent two angels to Sodom in order to warn Lot to get out. He in turn warned his daughters and their prospective (betrothed) husbands, but the two men scoffed (Gen. 19:14). So only Lot, his wife, and his two daughters left the city, and God then sent fire and brimstone down on Sodom and Gomorrah. Lot's wife yearned for "sin city" and suffered the consequences of judgment.

Fire and brimstone: These words have become synonymous in the English language with preaching that emphasizes hell and final judgment. This is quite proper; this is exactly what God's destruction of Sodom and Gomorrah is supposed to remind us of. But what Christians fail to recognize is the context of those fearful words. God was not raining fire and brimstone down on the heads of people as individuals; He was raining fire and brimstone down on a pair of cities. Individuals perished, of course, but they perished as members of cities whose sins had cried out to God for *collective judgment*. Abraham in his negotiating with God, had described God well: the Judge of all the earth.

God would have spared the two cities for the sake of as few as ten righteous people. But this was easy for God to agree to: There were not that many righteous people in those cities. The principle is clear, however: God is sometimes willing to spare a large number of evil people for the sake of a few righteous ones. It was so bad in Jeremiah's day, that God challenged him to locate a single righteous person: "Roam to and fro through the streets of Jerusalem, And look now, and take note. And seek in her open squares, If you can find a man, If there is one who does justice, who seeks truth, Then I will pardon her" (Jer. 5:1). God knew that Jeremiah would not find that person.

In Elijah's day, over a century earlier than Jeremiah, God promised the destruction of Israel, the northern kingdom. They would be destroyed by the sword, and carried into captivity. God promised to preserve seven thousand righteous people who would not bow the knee to Baal (1 Kings 19:18). In this case, there were not enough people in the land to save Israel from God's historic judgment. Still, this did not mean

that every righteous person would die. He would keep a handful of
them alive not many, but a few. In this case, He judged the collective, but
kept a remnant alive in the midst of the judgment. This, too, is God's way
of dealing with men in history. Israel was judged for the sin of one man,
Achan. Thirty-six men died because of one man's sin (Joshua 7:5). David's
sin of "numbering the people" brought judgment to the nation and the
death of "seventy thousand men of the people" (2 Sam. 24:15).

What God does is to look at those in authority. Are they righteous
men? If so, He is willing to delay His judgment for a season, for the sake
of the righteous leader, or even a few righteous residents. God delivered
Judah out of the hands of the army of Assyria, and the city did not fall
to the Babylonians until righteous King Hezekiah had died. Hezekiah
had prayed the prayer that God always honored in the Old Testament
era. He prayed that the army of the enemy would not capture the city,
so "that all the kingdoms of the earth may know that Thou alone, LORD,
art God" (2 Kings 19:19b). For this prayer, and also for the sake of the
memory of King David (v. 34), God spared His collective people from
external judgment. But His mercy lasted only for a few more years.
Then the prophet Jeremiah and other righteous people went into captivity in Babylon. "For out of Jerusalem shall go forth a remnant, and
out of Mt. Zion, survivors. The zeal of the LORD shall perform this" (v.
31). The judgment came: blessings (the survival of a remnant) and
cursings (captivity for all). There would be continuity (the survival of a
remnant and Judah's eventual return to the land) within discontinuity
(the enslavement of the people to Babylon and then to Medo-Persia).

The writings of the prophets are filled with judgments against the
nations. Isaiah warns the following nations of the judgment to come
after He is finished judging Israel: Assyria (Isa. 14:25–27), Philistia
(14:29–31), Moab (15–16), Damascus (17), Egypt (19), Tyre and
Tarshish (23). Indeed, the whole earth will be judged:

> Behold, the LORD lays the earth waste, devastates it, dis-
> torts its surface, and scatters its inhabitants. And the people will
> be like the priest, the servant like his master, the maid like her

mistress, the buyer like the seller, the lender like the borrower, the creditor like the debtor. The earth will be completely laid waste and completely despoiled, for the LORD has spoken this word. The earth mourns and withers, the world fades and withers, the exalted of the people of the earth fade away. The earth is also polluted by its inhabitants, for *they transgressed laws, violated statutes, broke the everlasting covenant.* Therefore, a curse devours the earth, and those who live in it are held guilty. Therefore, the inhabitants of the earth are burned, and few men are left (Isa. 24:1–6).

The prophet Obadiah warned Edom (the heirs of Esau) of coming judgment. Nahum warned Nineveh. Zephaniah warned Ammon and Moab, the heirs of Lot's incest (Zeph. 2:8–11). He also warned Ethiopia (2:12) and Nineveh (2:13–15). Jonah also warned Nineveh, and Nineveh's people believed and repented for a season. Jeremiah warned pagan nations, too (Jer. 46–51).

Everyone is guilty in Adam. God graciously allows men to live, and history to continue. But God can "call in men's debts" at any time. He has the legal right at any time to bring total judgment in history.

Collectives rise and fall as units, despite the fact that every member is personally responsible before God. The church is also a collective before God (1 Cor. 12), yet each member is fully responsible before God. The blessings and cursings of God fall on collectives (Deut. 28).

New Testament Judgments

It could be argued that in the New Testament, God's relationship with men has changed. Now He judges only individuals. But then how can we make sense out of the fall of the Roman Empire? Daniel prophesied that God's kingdom would crush the fourth empire, Rome:

You, O king, were looking and behold, there was a single great statue; that statue, which was large and of extraordinary splendor, was standing in front of you, and its appearance was awesome. The head of that statue was made of fine gold, its breast and its arms of silver, its belly and thighs of bronze, its legs of iron, its feet partly of iron and partly of clay. You continued looking until a stone was cut out without hands, and it struck the statue on its feet of iron and clay, and crushed them. Then the iron, the clay, the bronze, the silver and the gold were crushed all at the same time, and became like chaff from the summer threshing floors; and the wind carried them away so that not a trace of them was found. But the stone that struck the statue became a great mountain and filled the whole earth (Dan. 2:31–35).

What was the interpretation of the king's dream? Nebuchadnezzar, king of Babylon, was the head of gold, the greatest king. There would be three kingdoms after his, ending with the fourth, which was iron, breaking all other kingdoms and consolidating them in clay and iron (2:40–42). "And in the days of those kings the God of heaven will set up a kingdom which will never be destroyed, and that kingdom will not be left for another people; it will crush and put to an end all these kingdoms, but it will itself endure forever" (2:44).

Christ established His kingdom in history, as manifested by (but not encompassed by) the church. This took place during the Roman Empire. The fulfillment of this prophecy came as the Roman Empire disintegrated, rival emperors fought each other, and the church became the only institution with enough strength to pull society out of the chaos that Rome became. This happened three centuries after the cross. So God still deals with collectives as collectives in New Testament times, just as the prophecy of Daniel promised; "so the dream is true, and its interpretation is trustworthy" (2:45b).

Antinomianism

Those who deny that God judges collectives in the midst of time are arguing implicitly that God does not place nations and groups under His laws. It is an argument in favor of God's law over the actions of individuals, but not over collectives. It is an argument against biblical law: social (institutional), economic, cultural, and civil.

This sort of argument is not simply implicit in our day; it has become explicit. Christian intellectuals, especially in Christian colleges, repeat endlessly that the Bible offers no blueprints for society. Christians are regenerated, they say, but God has given His people no revealed standards or appropriate sanctions in the Bible. But what about the Old Testament standards and sanctions? These are no longer valid, the antinomians say.

Modern fundamentalists until very recently have argued the same way. Because of this, they long ago abdicated their role as God's representatives and ambassadors, and turned over the Christian colleges, Christian magazines, and other institutions to liberal intellectuals who have spent their academic lives defending the legal autonomy of today's covenant-breaking pagan antinomians, who are actually tyrants. The pagans have set the terms of debate in every field, and Christian antinomians have agreed with the pagans' starting point: The God of the Bible is irrelevant to the terms of discourse. A God who does not judge in history according to His law is irrelevant to history.

Sanctification

Moral regeneration is a necessary result of conversion. But how is it to be understood? We know that Christ died for the sins of all mankind, because only His death satisfied God's covenantal stipulations governing man. History went forward after Adam's sin only because God looked forward in time to the cross, and then He imputed this perfection of Christ's humanity, as well as His death and resurrection, back to all mankind. He does not bring all men to saving grace, but He certainly gives all men gifts that they do not deserve on their own merits. He brings rain and sunshine on all mankind (Matt. 5:45). He does this only because His wrath has been placated by Christ's work on the cross. Thus, God is "the Savior of all men, especially of believers" (1 Tim. 4:10b).

So all men are sanctified and set apart in history in the limited sense that *for a time*, they are set apart from God's perfect judgment. They are given time, what we can call a stay of execution. Christ's death and resurrection are the basis of this stay of execution for the covenant-breakers. Nothing else will suffice.

When a man is regenerated by God's grace (Eph. 2:8–10), God *imputes* Christ's perfection to him, not Christ's divinity, but His perfect humanity. God says, in effect, "I declare you not guilty, for I will look on My Son's perfect righteousness and His sacrificial death instead of looking at you." This is a *judicial act*. God *declares* us not guilty. He does so on the basis of Christ's *objective* fulfillment of God's *objective* law. Christ's moral perfection is therefore imputed to man. We call this perfection *definitive sanctification*.

Yet Christians still sin. Paul writes about running a good race (1 Cor. 9:24–26) and fighting the good fight (1 Tim. 6:12). Life is a struggle—a moral (ethical) struggle. We attempt in history to conform our lives progressively to the image of Christ's perfection. To deny that we are still sinners is to make liars of ourselves: "If we say that we have no sin, we are deceiving ourselves, and the truth is not in us" (1 John 1:8). This struggle, which is designed to improve our lives so that we will measure up to Christ's perfection, never ends until we die. We call this *progressive sanctification*.

Then, at the day of judgment, God declares us righteous again, and rewards us in terms of our works (1 Cor. 3:10–14). Of course, our ability to do these works is itself given to us by God's grace (Eph. 2:10). So there is final moral sanctification. We call this *final sanctification*.

We preach all three kinds of personal sanctification: definitive, progressive, and final. If we did not preach definitive sanctification, we could not explain how we pass from death to life, how God makes us new creatures. If we did not preach progressive personal sanctification, we could not explain why sin does not immediately kill us. We also could not explain the rewards God gives to each of us on the day of judgment because of our individual acts of righteousness. We need a doctrine of final sanctification to enable us to escape final judgment: God declares at the end of history that His gift of salvation to us was valid.

Collective Sanctification

Collectives do not have souls to bless or curse. Nevertheless, God judges nations in terms of how the people act. The collective sins of Sodom cried out to God. What else can this mean but that God decided that all the sins of Sodom, taken as a cultural unit, deserved judgment in history as a warning to future societies?

Each person has gifts and weaknesses. Each person's sins and successes are in terms of his gifts and environment, including his historical opportunities for good and evil. God judges us in terms of what we know, say, and do. This is what personal history is all about.

We use the same line of argument concerning collectives. Each society or separate (set apart) group has its specialized gifts and weaknesses. Each society's sins and successes are in terms of the collective gifts and environment in that society, including its historical opportunities for good and evil. God judges societies in terms of what its members know, say, and do. This is what national history is all about.

We recognize that some men are morally superior to others. The civil government (a collective responsibility, such as juries) punishes convicted criminals (individuals) for their sinful actions. Other people get rewards, such as medals or public praise. History therefore has meaning. It makes a difference in history how people live. This difference is reflected in the judgments of men and God in history.

We also recognize that some societies are better than others. One civil government punishes another (evil nations) in wartime for certain kinds of sinful actions. Other nations get rewards, such as military spoils or special trading rights. Historians write well of the victors.

Thus, we have to conclude that in some sense, God imputes Christ's righteousness to collectives. He certainly does this to the church. He presumably does this with nations. If he didn't, then why has He judged them in history the way He judged Sodom and Gomorrah? The blessings and cursings of Deuteronomy 28 include military victories (28:7) and defeats (28:25).

Ruler of the Nations

When we say that God rules the nations, we mean that He rules the nations *in history*. If so, then this means that God judges the nations in history. Any ruler who refuses to impose his judgment on those under his authority has abdicated. He has resigned his office. Or else he has died.

A few silly "intellectuals" shouted "God is dead" to the world for about two years, from 1966 to1968. It was not too long that many began to realize that such a proclamation also affirmed the death of man. A person does not challenge the God of the Bible unless he is suicidal. Man knows who God is, Paul writes in the first chapter of Romans, but man rebelliously worships the creature rather than the Creator (Rom. 1:18–23). So when men act as though God is dead, they call God's wrath down on them. They commit suicide. On the day that Adam ate of the tree of the knowledge of good and evil, he did surely die, and killed his posterity with him.

If we do not preach to men that God judges individuals, groups, and nations *in history* then we are adopting the false doctrine that God has abdicated His office and has stepped down from His throne. He may step back to His throne on judgment day, or sometime during an earthly millennium in which Jesus physically returns to rule visibly on earth, but until then, we are saying, "There is no heavenly ruler of the nations."

This leaves the office of judge open and the throne empty. Guess who will rush to the empty throne? Man. More specifically, power-seeking elitists who want to play God.

There must always be judgment in history. The question is: Whose? God's or man's?

Summary Concepts

We have to affirm the Triune nature of God. We have to affirm the equal ultimacy of the One and the Many. We have to affirm the reality of individuals and collectives. We therefore have to affirm the reality of God's judgments in history against individuals and collectives. This is the message of the covenant.

Sodom and Gomorrah were judged in the midst of their sins, in the midst of history. God sent no prophet to warn them. They were responsible before God for their sins, and in the midst of prosperity, the day of doom came upon them. God judges collectives. He will sometimes spare an evil collective for the sake of a few righteous people. But eventually judgment comes in history, and the righteous minority suffers.

The nations have broken God's covenant and have transgressed His law, Isaiah warned. Thus, they are always ripe for historic judgment. Their citizens may pretend that they do not recognize God's claim on them, but they cannot play pretend forever. Eventually, judgment comes.

Individualism denies the covenant. It denies that God judges collectives in the midst of time. Without covenant sanctions by God against nations, there can be no doctrine of covenant law over nations. Thus, individualism results in social antinomianism.

There must be sanctification of individuals: definitive, progressive, and final. There must also be sanctification of collectives: definitive and progressive, though not final (day of final judgment). This is the basis of all history, which includes individuals and collectives.

A God who does not bring judgments against nations in history is not the ruler of the nations. If He is the ruler of the nations, then He does bring judgment against individuals and collectives. He does so in terms of His laws that govern individuals and collectives.

Summary Points

1. God judged Babel, Sodom, and Gomorrah.
2. God therefore judged nations other than Israel.

3. Responsibility is collective.

4. God has promised in the past to protect a whole society for the sake of a few righteous people.

5. He spared Judah for the sake of one righteous king.

6. The prophets warned pagan nations that they should repent.

7. Individualism denies the covenant.

8. God judges only individuals on judgment day (Rev. 20:11–15).

9. He judges nations and groups within history.

10. A denial of collective judgment usually is accompanied by a denial of God's law for collectives.

11. Sanctification (God's setting apart morally) applies to individuals and also to collectives.

12. A measuring ruler is a tool of dominion; so is a governmental ruler. Both impose *limits*.

13. God judges nations in history for disobeying His limits.

14. God has not abdicated His office as ruler in history.

Call No Man Your Father

And do not call anyone on earth your father; for One is your Father, He
who is in heaven. And do not be called leaders; for One is your Leader,
that is Christ (Matt. 23:9–10).

Before the Bible can be used as the blueprint for civil government,
Christians must repudiate the promise made by politicians· "We will
take care of you."

God is the source of our protection. He alone can provide true
safety from invaders, criminals, famine, pestilence, and all the other
judgments that happen to men. Most importantly, He protects His
people from the final judgment of hell. God alone is our Father in heaven.
We have no father in Washington, London, Paris, or any other national
capital.

Most modern advocates of the "caretaker State," meaning the paternal State, believe that the only hope for mankind is the citizen's relin-
quishing of personal responsibility and handing more and more authority over to the "experts" who work in the bureaucratic halls of civil
government. Some have called this "womb to tomb" security. This is
the false security of the prison cell. Any society that seeks to substitute
the State for God will eventually find itself enslaved. There is no freedom apart from Jesus Christ and His saving grace. There is no freedom

apart from God's covenant. Our long-term security is assured by God when we are covenantally faithful. This is the fifth point of the biblical covenant: continuity. Only God shows mercy to His people for thousands of generations, *if they keep His commandments* (Ex. 20:6).

Our Father

It is no accident that God is called "Our Father." God, because He is our Father, gives us "life and breath and all things" (Acts 17:25). God is our Father by *creation*. The State has not called us into existence. (The State also cannot end our eternal existence, just our physical existence.) "Life, Liberty, and the Pursuit of Happiness" are not given to us by the State; rather, they are an "endowment," gifts from God's gracious hand to be *protected* and *secured* by the State. When the State refuses to do this, it becomes a thief, or an accomplice of thieves.

God is our Father because *He gives life and takes it away*: "Naked I came from my mother's womb, and naked I shall return there. The LORD gave and the LORD has taken away. Blessed be the name of the LORD" (Job 1:21). The State has nothing to give but that which it first takes.

God is our Father in that *His Words are our sustenance*. All the promises of provision made by the State are temporary: "Man shall not live on bread alone, but on every word that proceeds out of the mouth of God" (Matt. 4:4; cf. Deut. 8:3). Jesus cited this verse when the devil asked Him to turn stones into bread as a sign of His miraculous power. But Christianity is not based on magic; it is based on the Word of God. It is based on *ethics*, not manipulation of matter.

If we want earthly wealth, we are to work hard and faithfully, saving for the future, thereby seeking the kingdom of God in a lawful manner. This message is repeated over and over in the Book of Proverbs. There is no legitimate substitute, especially not theft. Yet today's society is based on the politics of theft: "Thou shalt not steal, except by majority vote." Such a view of civil government is immoral. God wants us to look to Him for provision, not to the State:

All the commandments that I am commanding you today you shall be careful to do, that you may live and multiply, and go in and possess the land which the LORD swore to give to your forefathers. And you shall remember all the way which the LORD your God has led you in the wilderness these forty years, that He might humble you, testing you, to know what was in your heart, whether you would keep His commandments or not. And He humbled you and let you be hungry, and fed you with manna which you did not know, nor did your fathers know, that He might make you understand that man does not live by bread alone, but man lives by everything that proceeds out of the mouth of the LORD. Your clothing did not wear out on you, nor did your foot swell these forty years. *Thus you are to know in your heart that the LORD your God was disciplining you just as a man disciplines his son* (Deut. 8:1–6).

Nearly every time the Israelites were in need of provisions, they wanted to go back to Egypt, back to the imagined security of what they believed was a fatherly State. When the freed Israelite slaves were hungry, instead of turning to God their Father for provision, they turned to the supposed security of tyrannical Egypt: "Would that we had died by the LORD's hand in the land of Egypt, when we sat by the pots of meat, when we ate bread to the full; for you have brought us out into this wilderness to kill this whole assembly with hunger" (Ex. 16:3). Their god was their appetite (Phil. 3:19): "For such men are slaves not of our Lord Jesus Christ but of their own appetites" (Rom. 16:19).

Finally, God is our Father in that He redeems us. In one sense, God is the Father of all. But in a very special sense, God is Father only to His adopted children. Jesus called the Pharisees children of their father the devil because they repudiated His redeeming work (John 8:31–47). We are adopted children who can now cry out, "Abba! Father!" (Rom. 7:15).

God Feeds Us

Even though God fed the Israelites in the wilderness, still they sought the supposed security of Egypt instead of the freedom and security they had with God as their Father. Even after God provided them the food they needed, they still grumbled. Egypt continued to seem attractive. "And the rabble who were among them had greedy desires; and also the sons of Israel wept again and said, 'Who will give us meat to eat? We remember the fish which we used to eat free in Egypt, the cucumbers and the melons and the leeks and the onions and the garlic, but now our appetite is gone. There is nothing at all to look at except this manna'" (Num. 11:4–6). They were, in essence, saying, "You can't beat security . . . three meals a day . . . a roof over our heads . . . steady work . . . . 'Slavery'? That's such an unpleasant word. . . . We always knew where our next meal was coming from. . . . That's security." A dog could say as much.

Did you catch what they said? They actually believed that these things had been "free" in Egypt. Free? They had been slaves! They had paid for these things with their own lives. A return to Egypt meant bondage to a system where they had no voice in the way they lived. There was no future for them in Egypt. The children of their children would be slaves, called into service to build a civilization to the glory of Pharaoh. Marching on to Canaan meant a promised land "flowing with milk and honey" where they could build a civilization based on the principles laid out in Scripture for the glory of God and as a beacon to the nations (cf. Deut. 4).

Slaves or Servants?

In both Hebrew and Greek, the word for "servant" is the same as the word for "slave." Yet we know that it is better to be a servant than a slave. What is the difference, biblically speaking?

All men are servants by nature. We are creatures made in God's image. We are made to serve God, and therefore we are made to rule in the name of God (Gen. 1:26–28), under the law of God (Deut. 8), always in light of the fact that we will be judged by God (Rev. 20:11–15). We are creatures, not the Creator. God alone is not a servant by nature. He is the Master by nature—His own self-existent nature.

What about slavery? *Slavery is the demonic imitation of service to God.* It is service to a creature, Satan, the enemy of God. He, too, seeks servants, but service to him necessarily involves bondage to sin. Those who reject God as loving Master will eventually seek another lord: Beelzebub, "lord of the flies." When men rebel against God, they are rejecting God as their Lord and Master. In doing so, they fall under the mastery of sin and ultimately under mere men as their rulers.

Slaves to the State

We should not expect God's covenant people to choose to be slaves to the State over freedom in Christ: "If therefore the Son shall make you free, you shall be free indeed" (John 8:36). The status that the Christian has is no longer one of slavery but of servant-sonship: "God has sent forth the Spirit of His Son into our hearts, crying, 'Abba! Father!' Therefore you are no longer a slave, but a son; and if a son, then an heir through God" (Gal. 4:6–7).

When the people reject God as their King, they once again adopt the slave mentality. They look for security outside of Christ. There are always powerful men who are ready, willing, and able to accommodate this evil search, and such men find their way to the exercise of power: the State. They seek and find willing political slaves. Instead of turning to God in repentance, "slave-mentality" people turn to political rulers for earthly security, even after God warns them of the consequences of their rejection of Him (1 Sam. 8:7).

A Prophet's Neglected Warning

What the Bible teaches is that *sin is the first step toward slavery.* The story of Israel is one long testimony of the truth of this cause-and-effect relationship. Israel never learned the truth of the story, and so God scattered them, again and again. Eventually, He took the kingdom from them and passed it on to a faithful remnant that included those once thought to be outside the covenant community (Matt. 21:43; Eph. 2:11–22; 1 Peter 2:6–10).

During the period of the Judges, all the governing institutions of Israel had become corrupt: from the individual in self-government, where "every man did what was right in his own eyes" (Judges 17:6), to the judges in civil government "who did not walk in [Samuel's ways], but turned aside after dishonest gain and took bribes and perverted justice" (1 Sam. 8:3). Even the priesthood was corrupt: "Now the sons of Eli were worthless men; they did not know the LORD and the custom of the priests with the people" (1 Sam. 2:12–13).

The corruption of the individual resulted in the inevitable corruption of family, church, and State. Instead of repenting and turning to God, they turned to Samuel and demanded a "king to judge us like all the nations" (1 Sam. 8:5). In making this demand, God told Samuel: "Listen to the voice of the people in regard to all that they say to you, for they have not rejected you, but they have rejected Me from being king over them" (1 Sam. 8:7). Their choice of security by repenting and turning to God as their Savior, Lord, and Provider was rejected. Instead, they turned to the false security offered to them by a civil government that would subject them to slavery in the name of security.

1. The king would raise an army for his purposes in opposition to the law (Deut. 20). Samuel told the people that war would be a way of life in Israel: "He will take your sons and place them for himself in his chariots and among his horsemen and they will run before his chariots" (1 Sam. 8:11). Instead of appearing before the LORD "three times a year" as part of God's army (Ex. 23:17), the men would appear before this king "like all the nations" (1 Sam. 8:5).

2. The king would use this army for personal profit: "He will appoint for himself commanders of thousands and of fifties, and some to do his plowing and to reap his harvest and to make his weapons of war and equipment for his chariots" (1 Sam. 8:12).

3. The young women of Israel would be subject to the whims and

fancies of the king: "He will take your daughters for perfumers and cooks and bakers" (1 Sam. 8:13). God cares and provides for his daughters (Ex. 3:22), while Saul abuses the daughters of Israel.

4. Private property will no longer be safe. The property and labor of others will be used to pay for political favors: "He will take the best of your fields and your vineyards and your olive groves, and give them to his servants" (1 Sam. 8:14). What belongs to God and is given to men as a stewardship under God (Deut. 6:10–11), Saul would steal in order to increase his power and influence over the nation (cf. 1 Kings 21).

5. The king would demand a tithe in taxation—a sign of tyranny, for only God can require a tenth: "He will take a tenth of your seed and of your vineyards, and give to his officers and to his servants" (1 Sam. 8:15),

Eventually the people "will cry out in that day because of your king whom you have chosen for yourselves, but the LORD will not answer you in that day" (1 Sam. 8:18).

Even after Samuel warned the Israelites that the king would be a tyrant, the people still wanted a king: "Nevertheless, the people refused to listen to the voice of Samuel, and they said, 'No, but there shall be a king over us, that we also may be like all the nations, that our king may judge us and go out before us and fight our battles'" (1 Sam. 8:19–20). But God was supposed to fight their battles, not a human king: "The LORD does not deliver by sword or by spear; for the battle is the LORD's and He will give you into our hands," David told Goliath (1 Sam. 17:47).

Our modern State operates in a similar way. Taxes are above forty percent. Some states have a *sales tax alone* that approaches ten percent. Add Social Security (FICA), gasoline, hotel, entertainment, excise, airport, property, and other hidden taxes.

The State's Job

What should civil government do? Are there specific tasks that the civil magistrate is required by God to perform? Certainly the State in the Bible is not pictured as a substitute father; rather, since the Fall, it is to be a judge "that does not bear the sword in vain" (Rom. 13:4).

The family, church, and State are authorities ordained by God to perform tasks in their prescribed jurisdictions. The family has no authority or power to perform the tasks commissioned by God for the church and the State. The church is not called on to supplant either the family or the State in their appointed tasks. The State has no authority over families or churches as they perform their God-ordained duties. Of course, if a family member commits murder, is tried and convicted, then the State is duty-bound to execute the murderer. But the church has a task to perform as well; it must "restore the brother" (Matt.18). These functions are not mutually exclusive. Prison chaplains have been part of our nation's penal system. A chaplain was often the last person a prisoner would see prior to his execution.

The State is God's "minister," taking vengeance out on those who do "evil" (Rom. 13:3–4). The State is the necessary ministry of social order. For example, the State probably has legitimate jurisdiction to build and keep up roads (Deut. 19:3) and enforce local land use contracts (Num. 35:1–8). But many believe we need a strong central government to guarantee the redistribution of income to provide for the economic welfare of all, the instruction of the citizenry through tax dollars and compulsory education laws, the subsidizing of failing business enterprises, and the capping of prices to "protect" the citizenry against "unfair" prices. In biblical terms, the State has no jurisdiction or authority to perform these functions.

If we believe the State is to be a substitute parent, then we must recognize that those who desire to create a State with this in mind will use the sword to see that their goals are enacted. The power of the sword will be used to exact the needed money to pay for these "free services."

More often than not, the State becomes an advocate for highly influential political groups. The tax money of the many is used to establish the goals of the few. Promises are made to citizens. For from their constituency, political favors are granted by those running for office. Of course, it's usually done under the slogan of "taxing the rich in order to help the poor." These political stepfathers set a trap for the dependent. In time, the politically dependent get "hooked" on the favors from a supposed benevolent State. Slavery is the result. The dependency habit is hard to break. More and more promises are made, and fewer freedoms are secured by civil law. Where individuals, families, and churches had authority and power, the State has now moved in and supplanted their God-ordained jurisdictions, all in the name of freedom, security, and greater efficiency. This is why the Bible is very specific as to what the civil magistrate ought to do. Before a nation will have good *civil* government, a nation must have good *self*-government.

Civil Justice

Let's establish the biblical guidelines for the operation of the State in society. First, civil government should operate judicial systems at the local, state, and national levels. The law of God, as outlined in Scripture, is to be the standard of justice. If the accused does not believe justice has been done, he can appeal his case to a higher court. He can move from a local jurisdiction to, say, the county, state, or a district court. Finally, he can appeal to the Supreme Court.

A judicial system can operate only as long as the majority of the citizenry are self-governed. Our nation's courts would be swamped and justice perverted if the majority were lawless. We are now seeing the breakdown in law and order, a backlog of court cases, and bulging prisons. Self-government is being repudiated by a growing segment in our nation.

Just Weights and Measures

Second, the State must ensure the maintenance of "just weights and measures." God considers tampering with weights and measures to be "violence and destruction" (Ez. 45:9). Men are not permitted even to *own* false weights and measures: "You shall not have in your bag differing weights, a large and a small. You shall not have in your house differing measures, a large and a small" (Deut. 25:13–14). Again, a biblical monetary system can only work when the people are self-governed, when they do not cheat, pilfer, falsely advertise, or appeal to their civil representatives to create laws that favor them.

When civil governments abandon laws related to economics, the people suffer. Devaluing the currency through inflation to fund non-biblical political projects, especially hurts the poor: "Your silver has become dross, your drink diluted with water. *Your rulers are rebels, and companions of thieves; every one loves a bribe, and chases after rewards. They do not defend the orphan, nor does the widow's plea come before them*" (Isa. 1:22–23).

Defending Christianity from Public Attack

Third, Christianity should be protected against its enemies. The State cannot be neutral toward the Christian faith. Any obstacle that would jeopardize the preaching of the Word of God and carrying out the Great Commission must be opposed by civil government. Civil rulers should have the interests of "godliness" and "dignity" in mind as they administer justice. This is why Paul instructs Christians to pray for their rulers, so "that we [Christians] may lead a tranquil and quiet life in all godliness and dignity" (1 Tim. 2:2).

Many wish to maintain that the State must be religiously and morally neutral. The Bible makes no such suggestion. Even our Constitution assumes the protection of the Christian religion. The First Amendment had the specific purpose of excluding all rivalry among *Christian* denominations. Paul expected even the Roman civil government to protect him from those who threatened the Christian religion (Acts 23:12–31; cf. 25:11). This means civil government cannot be religiously neutral. If the Christian religion is not defended, then some other religion will be, usually a State religion that degenerates into secularism. The State cannot be neutral toward all religions because all religious views or philosophies necessarily entail uncompromising moral systems, and this guarantees conflict with those of other religious systems. If the State were truly "neutral," it would enact no laws, for each law would penalize someone's religion or religious view or religious practice.

National Defense

Fourth, the civil magistrate, given that it has the power of the sword, is obligated to defend the nation against national and international aggressors, revolutionaries, and terrorists. Ultimate peace, however, can only be realized through the life-transforming gospel of Jesus Christ. Peace with God brings about peace with others: "Never pay back evil for evil to anyone. Respect what is right in the sight of all men. If possible, so far as it depends on you, be at peace with all men" (Rom. 13:17–18; cf. 5:1). Genuine and lasting peace will not come through law, a show of force, political promises or compromises, the elimination of poverty, worldwide "public education," or the establishment of a one-world humanistic government.

Praying for peace, as an aspect of self-government, is no substitute for the preaching of the gospel so that the nations are discipled according to the Word of Jesus Christ (Matt. 28:18–20). Wars are not the result of environmental factors. Rather, they are the result of man's inherent sinfulness: "What is the source of quarrels and conflicts among you? Is not the source your pleasures that wage war in your members? You lust and do not have; so you commit murder. And you are envious and cannot obtain; so you fight and quarrel . . ." (James 4:1–2).

Does this mean that a nation should not defend itself against the sinful military advancements of aggressive nations? The Bible takes evil and the reality of war seriously (Neh. 4:7–18; Eccl. 3:8; Joel 3:10; Matt. 24:6–7; Luke 11:21–22; 14:31–32); it recognizes that if men will war with God they certainly will war with other men. Under certain circumstances the individual is given the authority to attack and kill an intruder (Ex. 22:2). The civil magistrate is God's "avenger who brings wrath upon the one who practices evil" (Rom. 13:4). The civil magistrate's symbol of authority is the "sword," an instrument of temporal judgment. Israel was commanded to have an army of armed men (Deut. 20). While peace is what we all desire, war often is a reality we must face and prepare for.

Quarantine

Fifth, civil government has the power to quarantine, to protect human life. Plagues can race through whole populations because of the infectious nature of the diseases transmitted through casual and sexual contact. The individual with the infectious disease "shall live alone" (Lev. 13:46). Even his home can be "quarantined" after "an inspection" (14:33–53). If the disease is not abated, then even his house can be torn down (14:39–42). The State is given legislative power to deal with plagues, epidemics, venereal diseases, and other contagious and dangerous diseases like Acquired Immune Deficiency Syndrome (AIDS). Unfortunately, homosexuality, the biggest spreader of AIDS in developed countries, is a politically protected aberrant sexual lifestyle.

Defining and Defending Private Property

Sixth, civil government has the duty to protect private property. When individuals, families, churches, and business establishments possess property, they have an area of liberty and dominion that is beyond the reach of men with greater power and influence. The Bible is explicit about how property is to be acquired. Confiscation through State power is not legitimate. The commandments "You shall not steal" (Ex. 20:15) and "You shall not covet" (20:17) are meaningless unless there are prior owners who are secure in their right to hold the land. When Naboth refused to sell his land to king Ahab, the king devised a plot to kill Naboth in order to confiscate his land: "Arise, take possession of the vineyard of Naboth, the Jezreelite, which he refused to give you for money" (1 Kings 21:15).

Off Limits

A careful reading of Scripture will show that the State (civil government) has almost no authority to regulate education, business, welfare, and ecclesiastical affairs. For example, the only time education of children is taken on by the State is when the people of God are held captive by a pagan government (Dan. 1:1–7). Jurisdiction of education is given to parents (Deut. 6:4–9), not the State. A legitimate educational function of the State would be military academies. The State certainly has jurisdiction to punish fraudulent business practices, but it does not have the authority to determine who a business must hire or how much it should pay in wages.

Caring for widows is another concern. The responsibility first lies with family members. This is why Paul makes a distinction between "widows indeed," who have no family or who have families that refuse to care for them, and widows who have family members who can help out: "Honor widows who are widows indeed; but if any widow has children or grandchildren, let them first learn to practice piety in regard to their own family, and to make some return to their parents; for this is acceptable in the sight of God. Now she who is a widow, indeed, and who has been left alone has fixed her hope on God, and continues in entreaties and prayers night and day" (1 Tim. 5:3–5). The church is to step in and help those widows "who are widows indeed." Their hope is fixed "on God." The church is God's special representative on earth. God's provision comes through the church in tithes and offerings of the people. The State can best help widows by not taxing inheritances.

Some of Jesus' harshest words are for children who put their parents' lives in jeopardy. He pronounces the death penalty on unfaithful and self-righteous children who neglect caring for their parents: "You nicely set aside the commandment of God in order to keep your tradition. For Moses said, 'Honor your father and your mother'; and, 'He who speaks evil of father or mother, let him be put to death'" (Mark 7:9, 10). Notice that this law does not apply to infants and young children. Jesus applies the law to children who actually are in a position to jeopardize the life of their parents. The apostle Paul says that those who fail to care for their own family members are "worse than unbelievers" (1 Tim. 5:8).

The State is not called on to feed the hungry and clothe the naked except as wartime measures. You will not find instructions in the Bible that gives jurisdictional authority to the State to establish a wealth transfer welfare system. What the State ought to do is keep the market place open. This means the abolition of minimum wage laws that keep the less skilled from entering the work force; the reduction of taxes at all levels; the elimination of Social Security taxes on those just entering the work force (this alone would add more than 12% to their income to save and invest as they choose); phasing out Social Security for employers and employees already in the system; and the elimination of all entitlement programs that keep the poor dependent on the Parental State.

Summary Concepts

The fifth basic principle in the Biblical blueprint for government is that the State is not our father, provider, or savior. We're all looking for security. Security is not neccessarily a bad thing. God wants us to find security in Him. But when man rejects God as the only Sovereign Lord and Savior, he turns to some other "higher power" to fill the vacuum.

There are those who are convinced that a better society can be created and maintained by turning over nearly all authority, power, and jurisdiction to "benevolent caretakers of our souls." "God is not needed," they say. And we begin to believe it. "Just give us a little more power. ... A bit more jurisdictional authority. . . . All we need is a few more tax dollars to make this or that program better. . . . After this, you'll see the difference."

We do see the difference. The merchants of promise have an insatiable appetite for power and control. There is never enough money to do what they claim needs to be done. So they're back again for more money. In all of this God is rejected as our Father. The State no longer wields the sword. Rather, it becomes a benefactor, buying votes with the slippery voice of the promise and the transfer of wealth from the "haves" to the "have-nots."

How do these merchants of promise remain in office? We the people keep them there. The nation has chosen its god, and it's not Jehovah.

Christians have fallen into the trap of looking to the State as a substitute father, looking for sustenance. God is our Father. He cares for us. Turning to the State for every provision is a form of slavery. Civil

Government has a very limited role, defined by God in Scripture. To go beyond those biblical limits turns the State into God's competitor.

In biblical terms, the State is a "minister of God," serving God by promoting the good and punishing the evil doer. The State must ensure the maintenance of "just weights and measures." The Christian religion should be protected against those who would work to destroy it. The State has the responsibility to protect the nation against internal and external aggressors. The State has the power to quarantine.

The State, because it is limited by God, does not have unlimited jurisdiction. The State does not have biblical authority to educate or to confiscate income to fulfill some ill-conceived social agenda.

Summary Points

1. God is the source of our protection.
2. The State is not our ultimate protector.
3. The modern humanist State is worshiped today as the primary provider of safety.
4. God gives life and removes it.
5. God's Word sustains us.
6. Obedience to Biblical law is the basis of long-term prosperity.
7. The Israelites kept returning to the State for their protection.
8. God feeds us by providing all the necessary conditions for success.
9. All men are either slaves or servants.
10. A servant to God is a free man spiritually.
11. A servant to Satan is a slave spiritually.
12. Slavery is Satan's imitation of servitude to God.
13. Modern men are increasingly slaves to the State.
14. Sin is the first step toward slavery.
15. Samuel warned Israel against the kingly State.
16. The State's job is limited: bearing the sword (vengeance).
17. It is to dispense God's justice: punishing criminals.
18. It is to enforce honest weights and measures.
19. It is to defend Christianity from public attack.

20. It is to defend the nation from invasion.
21. It is to impose medical quarantines.
22. It is to define and protect private property.
23. It has little authority over other spheres of government, especially in the area of welfare.

Jesus Alone Possesses
Divine Rights

And on His robe and on His thigh He has a name written,
"KING OF KINGS, AND LORD OF LORDS" (Rev. 19:15).

W hen nations refuse to acknowledge God's universal government, He promises sure judgment: "Now therefore, O kings, show
discernment; take warning, O judges of the earth. Worship the LORD
with reverence, and rejoice with trembling. Do homage to the Son,
lest He become angry, and you perish in the way, for His wrath may
soon be kindled. How blessed are all who take refuge in Him" (Psalm
2:10–12). "Homage to the Son" has reference to the Lord Jesus Christ
and to His written Word. Jesus instructed His disciples to "make disciples of all the nations" (Matt. 28:19). Jesus' Great Commission will
result in the nations paying homage to Him, the Son, by observing all
He commanded (28:20).

Who is a king? In the Bible, the king is the one who lays down the
law. He possesses the sovereign authority to require all those under his
jurisdiction to obey. He tells them what they are allowed to do, and
then he polices their behavior. The heavenly King is the only king who

lays down the law to all men, and who is present with all men always, to see if they obey.

In the Old Testament, God did not reserve His commandments for just the nation of Israel and the church. Scripture makes it clear that all kings in Israel were to copy the law in the presence of the Levitical priests, so the rulers would be careful to observe every word of the law (Deut. 17:18–19)

Even nations outside Israel were required to follow the law as it was given to the nation Israel. This is a controversial statement. If the nations of the Old Testament world were supposed to obey God's civil law, then it becomes more difficult to argue that nations of the New Testament world are not under the same obligation. But what is the evidence that nations in the Old Testament were to be governed by God's law? The best evidence is this: *God judged them.*

Sodom and Gomorrah were destroyed because they broke the law of God (Gen. 13:13).

God commanded the prophet Jonah to preach to the Ninevites (Assyrians) because their wickedness had come up before God (Jonah 1:2). The reason is clear: "There shall be one standard for you; it shall be for the stranger as well as the native, for I am the LORD your God" (Lev. 24:22).

The prophet Amos set forth the coming judgment of God to Damascus, Gaza, Tyre, Edom, Ammon, and Moab. These non-Israelite nations were accountable for their transgressions: "For three transgressions . . . and for four I will not revoke its punishment" (Amos 1:3, 6, 9, 13; 2:1). Non-Israelite nations were to be judged along with Judah and Israel (Amos 2:4, 6). There is one law and one Lawgiver. The One who gives the law is the sovereign Lord of history: all of history, not just Israel's history and not just the church's history.

The Law Established

The New Testament shows a similar emphasis, as we should expect. The God of the New Testament is the God of the Old Testament.

We must not adopt a "two gods" view of history, with a mean, evil, tyrannical god in the Old Testament, and a sweet, kind, "devil may care, but I don't" god of the New Testament. God does not change (Mal. 3:6); therefore, His law does not change (Matt. 5:17–20).

Though Christians do not make blood sacrifices as remission for sins, we do keep this Old Testament law in Christ. We take holy communion, in which the wine becomes the sacrificial equivalent of His blood. The Bible states that "all things are cleansed with blood, and without shedding of blood there is no forgiveness" (Heb. 9:22; cf. Lev. 17:11). Shed blood is still required, but Jesus became our perfect and final sacrifice for sins by the shedding of His blood: "But now once at the consummation of the ages He has been manifested to put away sin by the sacrifice of Himself" (Heb. 9:26). All ceremonial laws, which look forward to the redemptive work of Christ, are fulfilled when an individual repents of his sin and unconditionally surrenders himself to Jesus.

The redemptive work of Jesus does not free us from an obligation to keep the moral and civil laws laid down in the Bible, however. Scripture shows no instance of an individual, Christian or pagan, who is free to ignore these laws. We are freed from the "curse of the law" (Gal. 3:13), but not from the guidance of the law: "Do we then nullify the Law through faith? May it never be! On the contrary, we establish the Law" (Rom. 3:31). Of course, the non-Christian is free neither from the curse of the law nor from its demands: "He who believes in Him is not judged; he who does not believe has been judged already, because he has not believed in the name of the only begotten Son of God" (John 3:18).

Turmoil that reaches our newspaper headlines can be traced to repudiating the saving work of Jesus Christ and denying His law as a standard for the nations. Man first sinned by rejecting the absolute government of God: Adam and Eve attempted to interpret life by their own standards. What is true for individuals is multiplied for the nations.

Christianity threatens all totalitarian regimes because the Christian citizen's ultimate allegiance belongs to God, who rules all earthly kingdoms and who calls those who rule to rule according to laws set forth in Scripture rather than by the whims of men.

Daniel's prophetic dream showed the nations that opposed the ordinances of God and their eventual destruction. The kingdoms were humanistic, anthropocentric (man-centered), kingdoms: "You, king, were looking and behold, there was a single great statue" of a man (Dan. 2:31). God brought an end to man's attempt to rule without His saving work and law structure by crushing the colossus: "Then the iron, the clay, the bronze, the silver and the gold were crushed all at the same time, and became like chaff from the summer threshing floors; and the wind carried them away so that not a trace of them was found" (2:35).

The Conflict Over Kingship

The Roman Empire presents a classic historical example of the Messianic man-centered State, of the denial of God's Law, and of the implementation of humanistic law. The Caesars declared themselves gods, and their decrees were acknowledged as the laws of gods. Because of each Caesar's false claim of divinity, his limited reign was threatened by God's unlimited and universal reign. Peter declared confidently that "there is salvation in no one else; for there is no other name under heaven that has been given among men, by which we must be saved" (Acts 4:12). The gospel of Jesus Christ, with its claim of divine prescriptions, threatened the very nature of the Roman State. Rome had to submit itself to the position of "minister" *under* God or be crushed by the power of God. Rome did not submit.

Early Christians were accused of "acting contrary to the decrees of Caesar, saying that there is another king, Jesus" (Acts 17:7). There is no evidence that the early church advocated that people act contrary to the prevailing law-system, except when those laws prohibited them from worshiping and evangelizing. However, those who heard the disciples preach understood the implications of Jesus Christ's demands. If Jesus is truly the Messiah, then even the State must submit to His authority and rule: no middle or neutral ground exists. Jesus' words make it clear that only one master can claim absolute authority: "No one can serve two masters; for either he will hate the one and love the other, or he will hold to one and despise the other" (Matt. 6:24).

The State *and* God cannot both be the absolute sovereign. One must submit to the other. Obviously, the State must submit to the Lordship of Jesus Christ or perish in its attempt to overthrow His rule. Any attempt by the nations to oppose the rule of God is an act of futility. God laughs at and scorns their attempts to overthrow the advancing kingdom of Christ (cf. Ps. 2).

"The LORD reigns," declares Scripture. Notice that the reign of God is comprehensive; it knows no geographical limitation: "Say among the *nations*, 'The LORD reigns'" (Ps. 96:10). God's reign is not limited to the nation Israel. Every nation is responsible to acknowledge the reign of God. Any attempt to deny God's reign will be met with judgment:

> Why are the nations in an uproar, and the peoples devising a vain thing? The kings of the earth take their stand, and the rulers take counsel together against the LORD and against His Anointed (*Messiah*): "Let us tear their fetters apart, and cast away their cords from us!" He who sits in the heavens laughs, the LORD scoffs at them. Then He will speak to them in His anger and terrify them in His fury (Ps. 2:1–5).

The fact that God's reign terrifies those who seek to free themselves from His rightful position as the reigning monarch of all creation: "Now therefore, O kings show discernment; take warnings, O judges of the earth. Worship the LORD with reverence and rejoice with tremblings" (Ps. 2:10–11). No nation can claim the exclusive title reserved for the Messiah of God. All civil governments are subordinate to God and are *under* His jurisdiction.

The Bible shows that "*the* government," the absolute reign of God, rests upon the shoulders of Jesus Christ (Isa. 9:6–7). This is not a future reign, but a present reality. The promise of government by the Messiah is realized at His birth: "For a child will be born to us, a son will be given to us; and the government will rest on His shoulders" (Isa. 9:6). Notice that "there will be no end to the increase of His government or of peace" (9:7). God then removes any nation standing in the way of the increase of the Messiah's government.

The nations do not influence God's decision on how He will evaluate them. The nations are in God's hands, and He controls them. Their conspiratorial desires to manipulate other nations are vain. Even Israel, God's chosen nation, is not favored when evaluated in terms of God's holy character (Matt. 21:33–46). Isaiah describes the perspective we need when considering the actions of the nations: they are nothing more than a drop in the bucket and dust on the scales compared to the grandeur, glory, and holiness of God (Isa. 40:15).

King by Nature

Jesus Christ is King because of who He is. Jesus has not overthrown another king to make His claim. He is King legally. God the Father has decreed Him to be king: "But as for Me, I have installed My King upon Zion, My holy mountain" (Ps. 2:6). God has anointed and sealed Him to His regal office. God has set the crown upon His head.

Jesus has a kingly title: "He is Lord of lords and King of kings" (Rev. 17:14; 19:16). He bears the ensigns of royalty: a crown (Heb. 2:9), a sword (Rev. 1:16; 2:16), a scepter (Heb. 1:8), and a coat of arms (Rev. 5:5). He is called "the ruler of the kings of the earth" (1:5). It is by Him that "kings reign" (Prov. 8:15). His throne is everlasting (Heb. 1:8). Even the angels worship Him: "And let all the angels of God worship Him" (1:6). He is the center of all that a person, family, church, group, organization or nation does. He is God, the Creator and Preserver of the Universe (John 1:1; Col. 1:17). He "upholds all things by the word of His power" (Heb. 1:2).

Confession

Because all actions originate in the heart (Mark 7:20–23; James 4:1), acknowledging Jesus Christ as King also must begin in the heart.

His kingdom is spiritual. He rules first in the hearts of men. This does not mean that He does not rule from on high, but the manifestation of His rule is supposed to be in deep. He sets up His throne where no earthly king does—in men's hearts. His sword, the Word of God, "is able to judge the thoughts and intentions of the heart" (Heb. 4:12). No nation can survive unless it acknowledges Jesus Christ as King, and its citizens embrace Him as such personally.

The Bible emphasizes that all people are Christ's subjects in a variety of ways: *First*, Jesus speaks to Nicodemus about the necessity of a "new birth," a comprehensive transformation of the entire individual (John 3:5–7). Man is not considered "sick." He is considered *sinful*. The unregenerate sinner is "dead in trespasses and sins" (Eph. 2:1). Only the regenerating power of the Holy Spirit can make a dead man live. The fundamental issue is ethical, not medical or psychological.

Second, the written Word of God is acknowledged as the only rule of faith and *practice*. Law is not found in the vote of the people, the decree of the courts, or the pronouncement of rulers. The law of God is Christ the King's law; therefore, it must be obeyed. Moreover, being set free in Jesus Christ liberates neither citizen nor ruler from the guidance, obligations, and benefits of the law (Rom. 3:31), only from the final curse of the law (Gal. 3:13). The consequences of broken law are well established (Deut. 28:15–68).

Third, the regenerate mind is renewed (Rom. 12:2). Prior to acknowledging Christ as King, all life is seen from man's perspective: "For as he [man] thinks within himself, so he is" (Prov. 23:7). The new creature in Christ should evaluate life from the perspective of the Word of God, thinking God's thoughts after Him, "taking every thought captive to the obedience of Christ" (2 Cor. 10:5).

Fourth, those who do not want Jesus as King "will wage war against the Lamb, and the Lamb will overcome them, because He is Lord of lords and King of kings, and those who are with Him are the called and chosen and faithful" (Rev. 17:14). The history of Rome's end is evidence that God is true to His word.

Separate Jurisdictions

The Bible reveals that the jurisdiction of the State and the jurisdiction of the church are to be separate, though the separation is not absolute. The Word of God transcends any absolute wall of separation some may seek to erect. For this reason, civil servants often are given religious titles. The king in Israel was the Lord's anointed set apart for a *civil* task in the same way the priest was set apart and anointed for his *ecclesiastical* (religious) task (Num. 3:3),

David, who was to replace Saul as the Lord's anointed, respected the special office of the king: "Far be it from me because of the LORD that I should do this thing to my lord [Saul], the LORD's anointed, to stretch out my hand against him, since he is the LORD's anointed" (1 Sam. 24:6).

Those subordinates who served with David also enjoyed religious titles. His chief officers were called *priests* (2 Sam. 8:18). These were not temple priests or Levites; they were comparable to *ministers* of Romans 13:4. The reason for the title "priest" is not immediately evident until we understand that these "priests," in their governmental role, were to give counsel to the king. Only the title of "priest" was significant enough to give these counselors' role the importance they deserved: they were to counsel the civil minister in godly law and actions. The New Testament emphasizes a similar title for all rulers by designating them as "ministers of God" (Rom. 13:4, 6).

King of All the Nations

Even outside Israel, rulers were given religious titles for civil functions. Cyrus is given the title of "shepherd." This title is usually reserved for God Himself (Isa. 40:11; cf. John 10) and the rulers of Israel (Jer. 23:4), but God calls a non-Israelite "My shepherd" (Isa. 44:28): "It is I who says of Cyrus, 'He is My shepherd! And he will perform all My desire.'" Cyrus is given an even more significant title: "Thus says the LORD to Cyrus His anointed, whom I have taken by the right hand, to subdue nations before him, and to loose the loins of kings; to open doors before him so that gates will not be shut" (45:1). The High Priest in Israel and the King are designated in the same way. Of course, it is the title for the coming deliverer, the "Messiah."

This means that rulers of the nations are given titles which clearly indicate that they are considered to be "ministers of God" (cf. Rom. 13:4, 6). Such special designations of "shepherd" and "anointed" tell us that even those rulers who do not seek to govern according to the law of God still are obligated to function in that capacity. Moreover, they will be held responsible for their actions.

The written Word of God is to be the standard for the king's rule in terms of civil matters: "Now it shall come about when he sits on the throne of his kingdom, he shall write for himself a copy of this law on a scroll in the presence of the Levitical priests. And it shall be with him, and he shall read it all the days of his life that he may learn to fear the LORD his God, by carefully observing all the words of this law and these statutes" (Deut. 17:18–19). The king, as well as his people, come under God's law.

The Divine Right of God Alone

No *biblical* "divine right of kings," in which the king was autonomous, a law unto himself existed in Israel. To possess such a divine right would have meant that the king's actions would have been autonomous; no one could have appealed to a higher court for justice since the king's edict was the law. The divine right of kings was the seventeenth-century's version of judicial humanism. It placed the king under God, but there was no human institution to call him to account. Thus, the divine right of kings under God became a theory justifying the autonomy of the king from any other human jurisdiction. It made the king the civil manifestation of God walking on earth. In theory, there could be no appeal beyond the king to God by means of any rival institution. But the theory claimed too much unregulated power for the king, and it sparked a revolution. By the end of the century in England, this theory regarding kings was tossed into the historical dustbin. The "Glorious

Revolution" of 1688 transferred the mythical divine right of kings to Parliament. Nine decades later, the American Revolution broke out in opposition to Parliament's taking seriously its own stolen theory.

One purpose of the civil law in the Old Testament was to see to it that the king's "heart may not be lifted above his countrymen" (Deut. 17:20). Citizens and king are to serve the same law. King Solomon prayed for "an understanding heart to judge [God's] people to discern between good and evil" (1 Kings 3:9). Solomon's standard of right and wrong was the Bible. Only when he ignored Scripture did judgment come to his kingdom. This is no less true in the New Testament, where Jesus is one with the Lord who gave Moses the law (John 10:30), and said that we are to keep His commandments (John 14:15; 15:14). By keeping Jesus' commandments, we keep the commandments of God, for Jesus is God (John 1:1).

God's standard of justice is the same for all His creatures. This includes nations that consider themselves non-Christian. Some people believe that because they do not acknowledge God as Lord and King, they somehow are exempt from following the law of God. Sodom and Gomorrah enjoyed no such exemption: "Now the men of Sodom were wicked exceedingly and sinners against God" (Gen. 13:13). This wicked city was destroyed for breaking God's law: in particular, the sin of homosexuality (19:4–5; Lev. 18:22; 20:13). Jonah went to preach to the non-Israelite city of Nineveh because of their sins. If the Ninevites were not obligated to keep the law of God, then how could they be expected to repent (Jonah 3)? The stranger, an individual *outside* the covenant community, must obey the law of God: "There shall be one standard for you; it shall be for the stranger as well as the native, for I am the LORD your God" (Lev. 24:22; cf. Num. 15:16; Deut. 1:16–17).

The law as given to Israel was a standard for nations surrounding Israel. When other nations heard of the righteous judgments within Israel, these nations remarked with wonder: "Surely this great nation is a wise and understanding people" (Deut. 4:6). The psalmist proclaims to the kings and judges of the earth "to take warning , . . and worship the LORD with reverence" and "do homage to the Son" (Ps. 2:10–11).

Quite frequently, the other nations are called upon in the Psalms to honor God. The prophets insisted that the nations surrounding Israel would respond to His threat of historical judgment. God does not exempt other nations from the requirements of His righteousness. He holds them responsible for their sins (Amos 1:3–2:5).

The New Testament Emphasis

The New Testament presupposes the moral order laid down in what we call the "Old Testament." John the Baptist used the law of God to confront Herod in his adulterous affair: "Herod . . . had John arrested and bound in prison on account of Herodias, the wife of his brother Philip, because he had married her. For John had been saying to Herod, 'It is not lawful for you to have your brother's wife'" (Mark 6:17, 18; Lev. 20:10; Deut. 22:22). This was not mere advice. John lost his own head in the exchange.

In Romans 13, the civil magistrate is termed a "minister of God" who has the responsibility and authority to punish evildoers. As God's servants these rulers must rule God's way. Just as a minister in the church is obligated to implement the law of God as it touches on ecclesiastical matters, a civil servant must implement the law of God in civil affairs. *The determination of good and evil must derive from some objective standard.* In Hebrews 5:14, the Christian is instructed to train his senses "to discern good and evil." In Romans 13:4 the civil authorities are to wield the sword, punishing evil doers and promoting the good.

God certainly does not intend the standard of good and evil to be simply whatever a ruler autonomously desires or thinks it ought to be. The standard of good and evil is nothing less than that which the Creator, Sustainer, Ruler, and Judge of heaven and earth ordains, decrees, and declares it to be: the revealed Word and law of God.

The psalmist declares he "will speak of Thy testimonies before kings, and shall not be ashamed" (Ps. 119:46). These testimonies are the "commandments" that he loves (119:47). Jesus informs His disciples that persecution will give them opportunity to speak "before governors and kings ... as a testimony to them and to the Gentiles" (Matt.10:18).

Civil servants approached John the Baptist regarding their obligations to the law of God: "Some tax-gatherers also came to be baptized, and they said to him, 'Teacher, what shall we do? And he said to them, 'Collect no more than what you have been ordered to.' And some soldiers were questioning him, saying, 'And what about us, what shall we do?' And He said to them, 'Do not take money from anyone by force, or accuse anyone falsely, and be content with your wages'" (Luke 3:13–14). John was not appealing to them on the basis of some "neutral" law, but referred to the sixth, ninth, and tenth commandments of the Decalogue, though he did not name them as such.

An incident in Jesus' ministry shows that biblical laws of restitution are still applicable. Zaccheus, an unscrupulous tax collector, followed the laws of restitution by promising to pay back those he defrauded: "If I have defrauded anyone of anything, I will give back four times as much" (Luke 19:8; cf. Ex. 22:1; Lev. 6:5). Christians are obligated to inform those who rule of the demands of the law and the consequences of disobedience. There is no area of life where man is exempt from the demands of the law of God.

Blessings and Curses

Because God's laws are a standard for all nations, consequences of disobedience affect pagan nations as well as godly nations. External blessings accrue to societies that conform to the laws of God, and there are curses for those societies that fail to conform externally to these laws (Deut. 28:1–68). The laws of God that relate to blessings and curses are operative for all peoples. The prophet Amos made this clear when he denounced the nations surrounding Israel. Damascus, Gaza, Tyre, Edom, Ammon, and Moab incurred the curses of Deuteronomy 28:15–63 (Amos 1:3; 2:5). Those judges who fail to render verdicts according to the absolute standard of the law of God "will die like men, and fall like any one of the princes" (Ps. 82:7).

The Levites stood before the people to remind them of their sins and the reason for God's judgment on their nation: "For our kings, our leaders, our priests, and our fathers have not kept the law or paid attention to Thy commandments and Thine admonitions with which Thou hast admonished them. . . . Behold, we are slaves today, and as to the land which Thou didst give to our fathers to eat of its fruit and its bounty, behold, we are slaves on it" (Neh. 9:34, 36). Slavery, in which even our bodies are ruled by despotic leaders (9:37), is the result of a nation's failure to keep the commandments of God.

Breaking God's commandments means "transgressors and sinners will be crushed together, and those who forsake the LORD shall come to an end" (Isa. 1:28). Harlotry, injustice, murder, theft, bribery, and affliction of the helpless are results of a nation's repudiation of God's laws and the adoption of man-made laws that have no moral justification given Darwinian assumptions about our evolutionary origins. Even the greatest kingdoms of the world will be reduced to dust if they fail to honor God's law (Dan. 2:31–35).

God in His providence appoints and deposes all rulers. He, therefore, is never surprised about the development of the nations because the heads of foreign powers are His servants. For example, Pharaoh (Rom. 9:17), Herod, and Pilate (Acts 4:25) were raised up by God to do God's will. The psalmist says that God "puts down one, and exalts another" (Ps. 75:7). God's dealings with Nebuchadnezzar surely are the most revealing actions of sovereignty brought upon an earthly ruler. Daniel acknowledges the sovereignty of God in the appointment and removal of kings by stating that God "changes the times and the epochs; He removes kings and establishes kings" (Dan. 2:21).

The rule and authority that men in power enjoy come from the gracious hand of God: "The Most High is ruler over the realm of mankind, and bestows it on whom He wishes, and sets over it the lowliest of men" (Dan. 4:17). Nebuchadnezzar was reminded of his rightful position as a ruler under God (4:25, 32). When the king came to his senses, God returned the kingdom to Nebuchadnezzar: "So I was reestablished in my sovereignty, and surpassing greatness was added to me" (4:36). This great lesson was not remembered, however. Some years later

Belshazzar's mockery of God's rule (cf. 5:2–4) brought sudden destruction, but not before Daniel reminded him of the nature of his sovereignty: "O king, the Most High God granted sovereignty, grandeur, glory, and majesty to Nebuchadnezzar your father" (5:16). Belshazzar's kingdom was "numbered," "weighed," "divided," and "given" by God (5:25–28).

Summary Concepts

The sixth basic principle in the Biblical blueprint for civil government is that the lordship of Jesus Christ is universal. There are no exemptions from God's service, including that of kings and all civil rulers.

One of the greatest lies ever fostered in the church is that Jesus is King of the church but not of the State. The law of God is valid for individual believers, but non-Christians are supposedly not required to keep it. The nations are supposedly under their own jurisdiction an assertion of their autonomy (self-law). The nations supposedly do not have to keep the law of God unless they wish to. God supposedly does not hold them accountable. Suppose, suppose, suppose: the theory is all supposition and no fact. It is a lie perpetuated by the devil and his minions.

If it were true, then it would mean that men around the world can break God's law and get away with it. Or, if His law does not bind them, then this theory means that God is not sovereign over the nations. Legal theory of all societies recognizes this principle: *no law-no authority, no law-no sovereignty*. Those who argue that God's law does not apply are in principle denying the sovereign rule of God.

This must be Satan's favorite lie. It is certainly one of his most successful lies in Christian circles.

You cannot come away from a reading of the Bible with the conclusion that the nations are exempt from the commandments of God. If the nations are exempt as long as they do not submit to Jesus as their King, then how will they be held accountable on judgment day? According to this "new theology," there is no accountability. The atrocities of despots from the beginning of time are off the hook.

Our country's foreign policy makes it evident that we have forsaken the gospel for the nations. When is the last time (let alone the first time) that you heard that what our foreign policy really needs is the claims of Jesus Christ? Do our ambassadors call the Russians, the Czechs, the Chinese, the Japanese, the Iranians, the Poles, and the Jews to surrender unconditionally to the lordship of Jesus Christ? This is the only hope for the world. God will not honor our supposed religious neutrality for long.

God establishes nations by His eternal decree. All nations are accountable to God and His law. When God is rejected as the King, false king-messiahs claim to be saviors of the people. The State and God cannot claim to be the ultimate sovereign. All conspiratorial designs of men and nations are doomed to fail.

Jesus is King of kings because of who and what He is. For nations to submit to Jesus as King, the gospel must be preached and the Word of God proclaimed as law. Both church and State are obligated to keep the law of God. The State cannot exempt itself from keeping the commandments of God except at its own peril.

There is a jurisdictional separation between church and State but not a religious separation. Jesus is King of all the nations. There is no "divine right of kings." The New Testament repeats the fact that Jesus is Ruler of the Nations. There are blessings and curses attached to obedience and disobedience.

Summary Points

1. God promises to bring judgment against nations that ignore His law.
2. New Testament nations are as bound by God's law as Old Testament nations were.
3. The God of the Old Testament is the God of the New Testament.
4. The Redemptive work of Christ has not freed us from obedience to God's law.

5. God's law threatens totalitarian nations.

6. God destroys all rival earthly kingdoms.

7. The Roman Empire fell because it opposed God and His church.

8. The early Christians were persecuted because they claimed that Christ was sovereign over all kings.

9. The State and God cannot both be equally sovereign.

10. The government rests on Christ's shoulders.

11. Christ is King legally.

12. The confession that Jesus is Lord must begin in the heart.

13. The jurisdictions of church and State are separate.

14. The civil magistrate is described using terms that denote a ministerial function.

15. Only God possesses divine rights.

16. Divine rights means not being subject to a legal appeal for one's actions.

17. In the past, king and parliaments have claimed divine rights.

18. This doctrine leads to tyranny.

19. God alone is king.

20. The New Testament says that all magistrates are under God's kingship.

21. God's law rules magistrates, and they are supposed to rule their subjects in terms of God's law.

22. Armed with God's law, the early church challenged the State.

23. The Levites were to warn kings against transgressing God's law.

24. Slavery results when rulers ignore God's law.

25. God still appoints all rulers.

We Must Render
Appropriate Service

Render to all what is due them: tax to whom tax is due;
custom to whom custom; fear to whom fear; honor to whom honor
(Rom. 13:7).

As we saw earlier, God has established a bottom-up system of multiple hierarchies: church, family, and State. This means that we must always be obedient *where obedience is required by God's law*. The appeals court system of Exodus 18 is a good guide: We are free men only when we obey God, and we must subject our actions to scrutiny by lawful, God-ordained, covenantal authorities in church, State, and family. The Bible instructs us to submit to *every* human institution. "Whether to a king as the one in authority, or to governors as sent by him for the punishment of evildoers and the praise of those who do right" (1 Peter 2:13). While Peter has *civil* authority in mind here, this text also includes family and church authorities. As Bible-believing Christians, we must always remember that when we speak of authority, we mean more than just *civil* authority.

The family has real authority that it exercises over its members:

"Children, obey your parents in the Lord, for this is right" (Eph. 6:1). The symbol of authority is the rod of correction: "He who spares his rod hates his son, but he who loves him disciplines him diligently" (Prov. 13:24). It is in the family that children ought to learn the basics of biblical authority and its relationship to church authority, the authority that an employer has over an employee, and the authority the police have over the citizenry within the confines of the law. The church has real authority to discipline members:

> And if your brother sins, go and reprove him in private; if he listens to you, you have won your brother. But if he does not listen to you, take one or two more with you, so that BY THE MOUTH OF TWO OR THREE WITNESSES EVERY FACT MAY BE CONFIRMED. And if he refuses to listen to them, tell it to the church; and if he refuses to listen even to the church, let him be to you as a Gentile and a tax-gatherer. Truly I say to you, whatever you shall bind on earth shall have been bound in heaven; and whatever you loose on earth shall have been loosed in heaven (Matt. 18:15–18).

The apostle Paul goes so far as to put ecclesiastical authority on an equal par with the civil courts: "Does any one of you, when he has a case against his neighbor, dare to go to law before the unrighteous, and not before the saints? Or do you not know that the saints will judge the world? And if the world is judged by you, are you not competent to constitute the smallest law courts?" (1 Cor. 6:1–11). The symbol of the church's authority is the "keys of the kingdom of heaven" (Matt.16:19).

Civil rulers, as well as family and ecclesiastical rulers, are called "ministers of God." The word "minister" in Romans 13:4 is the same word used for deacon and servant (see 1 Tim. 3:8). The symbol of the civil magistrate's authority is the "sword" (Rom. 13:4). This means that only the civil magistrate has the legitimate authority of capital punishment.

Resisting Tyranny

Rulers should not be cursed by the people: "You shall not curse God, nor curse a ruler of your people [because he represents God]" (Ex. 22:28; cf. Rom. 13:1). This does not mean, however, that the sinful practices and policies of rulers either represent God or should go unnoticed and therefore unchallenged (cf. Mark 6:18). Moreover, Christian citizens are under obligation to disobey those laws that prohibit worship and the proclamation of the gospel (Dan. 3; Acts 4:18; 5:29). In addition, a law that forces people to commit a crime, such as murder, must also be disobeyed (Ex. 1:15–22). Jesus made it clear that evil rulers must be exposed publicly as evil rulers (cf. Luke 13:32).

Old Testament Examples

The Hebrew midwives were commanded by "the king of Egypt" to put to death all the male children born to the Hebrew women (Ex. 1:15–16). They disobeyed the edict of the king: "But the midwives feared God, and did not do as the king of Egypt had commanded them, but let the boys live" (1:17). God shows His approval of their actions: "So God was good to the midwives, and the people multiplied, and became very mighty. And it came about because the midwives feared God, that He established households for them" (1:20–21).

Jochebed, Moses' mother, also disobeyed the edict of the king by hiding her child and later creating a way of escape so he would not be murdered by the king's army: "But when she could hide him no longer, she got him a wicker basket and covered it over with tar and pitch. Then she put the child into it, and set it among the reeds by the bank of the Nile" (2:3). Jochebed even deceived Pharaoh's daughter into believing that she was in no way related to the child (2:7–9).

Rahab hid the spies of Israel and lied about their whereabouts. When a route for escape became available, she led them out a different way from that of the pursuing soldiers. She is praised by two New Testament writers for her actions: "By faith Rahab the harlot did not perish along with those who were disobedient, after she had welcomed the spies in peace" (Heb. 11:31). Rahab is listed with Abraham as one whose faith was reflected in her works: "And in the same way [as Abraham] was not Rahab the harlot also justified by works, when she received the messengers and sent them out by another way?" (James 2:25). By sending the spies out by another way, she subverted the king's desire to capture the spies.

Shadrach, Meshach, and Abednego refused to follow the command of the king to worship the golden statue: "These men, O king, have disregarded you; they do not serve your gods or worship the golden image you have set up" (Dan. 3:12). When the three were thrown into the furnace, the angel of the Lord came to their aid (3:25).

King Darius signed a document that prohibited anyone from making "a petition to any god or man besides" himself (6:7). Anyone refusing to obey the order "shall be cast into the lion's den" (6:7). Daniel refused to obey. The Bible states that Daniel went out of his way to disobey the order: "Now when Daniel knew that the document was signed, he entered his house (now in his roof chamber he had windows open toward Jerusalem); and he continued kneeling on his knees three times a day, praying and giving thanks before his God, as he had been doing previously" (6:10).

New Testament Examples

The New Testament has similar accounts of resistance to tyranny. When Peter and John were ordered by the rulers and elders of the people to stop preaching in the name of Jesus (Acts 4:18), the two apostles refused to follow the prohibition: "Whether it is right in the sight of God to give heed to you rather than to God, you be the judge; for we cannot stop speaking what we have seen and heard" (4:19–20). Peter and John could not stop speaking what they had seen and heard because they had been commanded by Jesus to preach in His name (cf. Matt. 28:18–20; Acts 1:8; 1 Cor. 9:16).

On another occasion, some of the apostles were arrested for preaching and healing in the name of Jesus. Again, they were put in a "public jail" (Acts 5:18). During the night "an angel of the Lord . . . opened the gates of the prison" and commanded them to disobey the rulers of Israel: "Go your way, stand and speak to the people in the temple the whole message of life" (5:20). When the apostles again were confronted with the command not to preach and teach, their response was quick and sure: "We must obey God rather than men" (5: 29).

The apostles' obedience to God conflicted with the laws of the State. This resulted in the first apostolic death: "Now about that time Herod the king [Agrippa I] laid hands on some who belonged to the church, in order to mistreat them. And he had James the brother of John put to death" (Acts 12:1–2). Peter was later arrested for similar "crimes" against the State (12:3). God even sent one of His angels to release Peter from prison (12:6–8). There are several such cases where divine assistance released outspoken Christians from the hands of the State.

Praying for Civil Servants

Rulers need our prayers. *First,* to give them support for the difficult tasks that surely burden them. The work of the civil magistrate is multi-faceted. There are constant pressures that weigh heavily on the office of each civil representative. A minister in the civil sphere must keep his own house in order as well as the house of State. Family responsibilities are often neglected for the supposed urgency of civil affairs. There is the constant barrage of special interest groups wanting to turn the civil sphere of government into a vehicle to engineer society through power and coercion. The temptation to appease these groups is great.

Second, to have God change their minds when they stray from the principles of Scripture. I can remember talking with a congressman about the abortion issue. He told me that he would not change his mind no matter what argument he heard. This is certainly presumptuous and arrogant. The Christian is assured that God is in control of the king's heart: "The king's heart is like channels of water in the hand of the LORD; He turns it wherever He wishes" (Prov. 21:1). There is a Biblical precedence for this attitude. Pharaoh would not listen to the arguments of Moses. God made Pharaoh a believer (Ex. 3–15).

Third, to give them wisdom in applying the absolutes of God's Word to civil situations. This was Solomon's prayer, although sometimes he did not heed his own advice (1 Kings 3).

Fourth, to pray for a well-ordered State so the church of Jesus Christ is protected and given freedom in preaching the gospel (1 Tim. 2:1–4). The State must protect the *Christian* religion. Any obstacle that would jeopardize the preaching of the Word of God in carrying out the Great Commission must be removed by civil government. The apostle Paul instructs Christians to pray for those who rule so "that we [Christians] may lead a tranquil and quiet life in all godliness and dignity" (1 Tim. 2:2). Paul appeals to the civil magistrate for protection from those who were threatening the Christian religion (Acts 23:12–31; cf. 25:11).

Instructing Civil Rulers

Jesus told His disciples that they would be "brought before governors and kings for His sake" (Matt.10:18). The apostle Paul declared, "Woe is me if I do not preach the gospel" (1 Cor. 9:16). When Paul was brought before the civil officials of Rome, he was obligated, for he was under compulsion by God, to preach the gospel. King Agrippa was confronted with the claims of Jesus Christ and responded by saying, "In a short time you will persuade me to become a Christian" (Acts 26:28). Paul responds by saying, "I would to God [lit., *I pray to God*], that whether in a short or long time, not only you, but also all who hear me this day, might become such as I am, except for these chains" (26:29).

It is not enough to have "conservative" rulers who merely follow after the traditions of men. Christians should be working for *Christian* leaders whose lives are conformed to the image of Jesus Christ by the Word of God. Moreover, Christians must preach the whole counsel of God to all men, including civil rulers.

Civil governments have the responsibility to punish evil doers and promote the good. The task of civil government at all levels is to exercise its authority its jurisdictional authority and settle disputes between conflicting jurisdictions. When disputes and/or crimes are committed, the State must act swiftly and justly. The standard of judgment is the Word of God: "For it [the God-ordained authority] is a minister of God to you for good" (Rom. 13:4). Notice that Paul declares that the State is a minister for good. Paul has a biblical moral order in mind when he speaks about the operation of the State as minister.

In the Old Testament, the priests who were experts in the law of God instructed the king on how he should apply the details of the law to various civil issues (Deut. 17). Unfortunately, the church no longer sees its calling as prophetic.

Pursuing Peace

Peace can only be realized through the life-transforming gospel of Jesus Christ. Genuine and lasting peace will not come through law, force, political promises or compromises, the elimination of poverty, the establishment of a one-world humanistic government. To pray for peace, as we are instructed to do, can be no substitute for the preaching of the gospel so that the nations are discipled according to the Word of Jesus Christ (Matt. 28:20). Wars do not come because of environmental factors. Rather, they are the result of man's inherent sinfulness: "What is the source of quarrels and conflicts among you? Is not the source your pleasures that wage war in your members? You lust and do not have; so you commit murder. And you are envious and cannot obtain; so you fight and quarrel" (James 4:1–2). If this is true of the Christian community, should we expect anything less among non-Christians?

Rendering to Caesar

Because civil governments are ordained by God and act in a ministerial capacity, they are in need of revenue to carry out their jurisdictional role. Jesus states that Caesar is due tax money because he offers them protection against foreign enemies. Caesar renders a service: "Render to Caesar the things that are Caesar's; and to God the things that are God's" (Matt. 22:21). Jesus certainly was not endorsing the way Caesar governed in all cases, but He was, at least, upholding the biblical institution of civil government and its authority to limited taxation. Of course, those "things that are Caesar's" are not his by right just because he says so. Rather, they fall within the parameters of God's ordination of Caesar's jurisdiction. Jesus was not giving *carte blanche* authority to Caesar as the civil representative of the State.

Unfortunately, as civil government's role has expanded, so has its appetite for taxes. George Harrison, one of the founding members of the *Beatles*, described it this way in "Tax Man":

Let me tell you how it will be
There's one for you, nineteen for me.

(Refrain) 'Cause I'm the Tax Man, yeah, I'm the Tax Man

Should five percent appear too small,
Be thankful I don't take it all

(Refrain) 'Cause I'm the Tax Man, yeah, I'm the Tax Man

If you drive a car, I'll tax the street.
If you try to sit, I'll tax your seat.
If you get too cold, I'll tax the heat.
If you take a walk, I'll tax your feet.

(Refrain) 'Cause I'm the Tax Man, yeah, I'm the Tax Man

Don't ask me what I want it for
If you don't want to pay some more.

(Refrain) 'Cause I'm the Tax Man, yeah, I'm the Tax Man

Now my advice for those who die. Tax Man!
Declare the pennies on your eyes. Tax Man!

(Refrain) 'Cause I'm the Tax Man, yeah, I'm the Tax Man
And you're working for no one but me. Tax Man!

As a middle-class kid growing up in England, taxes were what other people paid. When he began to make lots of money, Harrison realized how oppressive the government was in its insatiable appetite for tax revenue.

For the Romans, lordship was personified in the Emperor. For the Jew, therefore, paying taxes was believed to be an acknowledgment that Caesar was a god. This is made clear by the stamp of the emperor's face on the coin of the realm and this declaration: "TI[berius] CAESAR DIVI AUG[usti] F[ilius] AUGUSTUS," or, in translation, "Tiberius Caesar Augustus, son of the deified Augustus." The Jews knew whose coin it was. It was used to pay taxes, and it was the medium of exchange throughout the Roman world. Israel benefited from roads, a Mediterranean Sea free of pirates, and a common silver currency unit. Why, then, should the Jews refuse to pay taxes to the State that provided these benefits? Why shouldn't they pay the tax? Why not admit that Caesar was the rightful civil ruler? It was from him that they derived their own civil protection. The Jews believed that paying a tax with the image of the emperor was akin to idolatry. But it was God's way of saying that their disobedience led them to submission under a foreign power,.

Supporting Godly Leadership

Moses chose leaders who had already come through the ranks of family, business, and community leadership: "Choose wise and discerning and experienced men from your tribes, and I will appoint them as your heads" (Deut. 1:13). The responsibility for choosing godly leaders rested with the people. Moses then chose from those who were presented to him as worthy leaders: "So I took the heads of your tribes, wise and experienced men, and appointed them heads over you, leaders of thousands, and of hundreds, of fifties and of tens, and officers for your tribes" (1:15). Judges were chosen with the same ethical and experiential considerations (1:16–17).

Today, Christians have the freedom and duty to vote for responsible leadership using the standard of God's law as the measuring device for their political choice: "By the blessing of the upright a city is exalted, but by the mouth of the wicked it is torn down" (Prov. 11:11). There is a direct relationship between those who rule and the condition of the nation: "When the righteous increase, the people rejoice, but when a wicked man rules, people groan" (29:2). Christians who refuse to vote, for whatever reason, are getting what their non-vote brings.

Qualified to Lead

The qualifications for leadership are ethical and practical, that is, they are to have some leadership experience in the family, church, school, or business world. Rulers must be "men of truth, those who hate dishonest gain" (Ex. 18:21). The standard by which they are to rule is not to be their own, and no amount of monetary and political gain will move them from their allegiance to God and His Word. They are to "fear God." This is the ethical dimension.

The apostle Paul builds on these principles when he sets forth the qualifications of leadership in the church. Ethical considerations abound. Self-government must first be manifested in a potential leader. Leaders must be able to control their own appetites (1 Tim. 3:1–7); that is, they must be self-disciplined in all their affairs. Paul draws on the Old Testament system of government that applied to both church and State, and he carries these principles to the New Testament people of God.

In addition to ethical qualifications, there are practical considerations as well. The individual who is scrupulous in personal, family, and business affairs will gain positions of leadership where experience is cultivated. Those who are faithful in small things (an ethical evaluation) will be entrusted with greater responsibilities (a practical result) (Matt.

25:23). This is why the young are discouraged from holding positions of authority without some supervision or accountability. New converts are susceptible to conceit because they have not gained the needed maturity to work out the implications of their new faith in Christ (1 Tim. 3:6).

Jethro's advice to Moses is that "able men" must rule (Ex. 18:21). Ability is cultivated through time as the Word of God is applied to life's situations. We must remember that while Timothy is told, "Let no one look down on your youthfulness" (1 Tim. 4:12), Paul was his mentor. Timothy was learning leadership skills under the tutelage of an experienced leader. Civil leadership, like ecclesiastical leadership, is designed to be ministerial. Those in authority must follow the pattern of God as *ministers* rather than attempt to define the role of governmental leadership in terms of how others rule (Luke 22:24–30; cf. 1 Sam. 8:5).

Summary Concepts

Civil government is not a "necessary evil." God established the civil sphere of government like He established the family and church, for our good. What ruins the goodness of these governments is the lack of godly leadership. We're often faced with voting for the best of two bad choices. It's hard to find men of principle, men who "fear God rather than man."

But where is leadership cultivated? The family and church are the training grounds for developing true civil servants. The example of Christ as the servant *par excellence* is our model. Most governmental leaders are persuaded by their voting constituency. If the people back home want some law passed that will favor their district or them personally, their congressman will seek out their wishes and vote accordingly. Service in the biblical sense means responsibility. Too many politicians are slaves to the will of the people. Their impetus for action is not principle but pressure.

The Bible commands us to submit "to every human institution." Governments are established by God, therefore, they rule in God's name. This is why rulers should not be cursed by the people. The Bible, however, shows resistance to tyranny is legitimate and is often commanded. Christians are commanded to pray for those in authority over them.

Civil rulers must hear from the Christian citizenry. Christians inherit the earth because we are "fellow-heirs with Christ." We have a stake in the way our world is being run.

Peace can only be realized when we recognize that we are first at war with God and need to be reconciled to Him. The State has the duty to collect taxes for its biblically defined function.

Christians should support qualified Christian leaders.

Summary Principles

1. God has established multiple covenantal authorities.
2. These authorities are structured as appeals courts, as in Exodus 18.
3. Civil authority is only one authority among many.
4. The family and the church can lawfully discipline its members.
5. The symbols of the church's authority are the keys to the kingdom.
6. The symbol of the State's authority is the sword.
7. The symbol of the parent's authority is the rod.
8. We must disobey laws that prohibit the public preaching of the gospel.
9. The Hebrew midwives disobeyed Pharaoh.
10. Moses' mother disobeyed Pharaoh, and saved Moses in an ark.
11. Rahab disobeyed the laws of Jericho by hiding the spies and lying to the authorities.
12. Shadrach, Meshach, and Abednego disobeyed Nebuchadnezzar's command to worship his statue. Daniel disobeyed the king and continued to pray three times a day.
13. Peter and John refused to obey the order to cease preaching.
14. Civil resistance must not be autonomous.
15. Christians are to pray for rulers: to guide them, to turn their hearts from evil, to judge society in terms of biblical law, and to achieve peace,
16. Christians are to instruct civil rulers in the law.

17. Civil government is required to enforce God's law.
18. Man cannot save himself.
19. The State cannot save man.
20. Civil governments are service institutions: service to God.
21. We owe taxes to the State.
22. Caesar's claims on us are not unlimited.
23. High taxes are one way God judges sin.
24. Leaders should be elected because of their righteous behavior.

Neutrality Is A Myth

No one can serve two masters; for either he will hate the one and love the other, or he will hold to one and despise the other   (Matt. 6:24).

The early Christians were accused of turning "the world upside down" (Acts 17:6). In one sense, those pagans who were negatively affected by the preaching of the gospel were correct in their assessment of how Christianity changed their culture.   The gospel's consistent critique of their worldview revealed the emptiness of their godless, humanistic, and decaying world. These unbelievers understood the implications of the gospel. The Christians "act contrary to the decrees of Caesar, saying that there is another King, Jesus" (17:7). Caesar or Christ? Man or God? The State or the Kingdom?

First-century humanists saw that their world was jeopardized by the claims and demands of Jesus Christ: "And His voice shook the earth then, but now He has promised, saying, 'Yet once more I will shake not only the earth, but also the heaven.' And this expression, 'Yet once more' denotes the removing of those things which can be shaken, as of created things, in order that those things which cannot be shaken may remain" (Heb. 12:26–27). God's kingdom "cannot be shaken" (11:28).

In another sense, these first-century humanists were wrong. Their worldview assumed that a godly order must be upside down. In reality, a Christian world order is right side up. Society does not function properly unless the effects of God's Word permeate every corner of culture. At this moment, the world appears upside down–*ethically* upside down. The Christian's task, through God's powerful provision in the gospel, is to turn it right side up.

In and Over the World, but Not of the World

Many Christians have refused to bring the first-century Christian faith into the twenty-first century. Often they are confused when they read Jesus' words, "My kingdom is not of this world" (John 18:36a). Jesus did not say His kingdom does not operate *in* this world. He did not say His kingdom is not *over* this world. When Jesus states His "kingdom is not *of* this world," He emphasizes the *origin* of His kingdom's power and authority. God's kingdom does not derive its authority from the world. His disciples had scattered. There was no army following Jesus. This should have been obvious to Pilate, "If My kingdom were of this world, then My servants would be fighting, that I might not be delivered up to the Jews; but as it is, My kingdom is not of this realm" (John 8:36b).

Caiaphas, the high priest, interrogated Jesus on *religious* questions. He wanted to know if Jesus was "the Christ, the Son of God" (Matt. 26:63). This did not concern Pilate. In fact, in order to have Pilate hear the grievances of the religious leaders, a *political* threat to Rome had to be fabricated: "And they began to accuse Him saying, 'We found this man misleading our nation and forbidding us to pay taxes to Caesar, and saying that He Himself is Christ, a King'" (Luke 23:2). Unless Jesus was portrayed as a political threat to the Roman Empire, they knew Pilate would not hear their case.

Pilate's question about kingship and kingdoms concerned political power. Jesus was questioned from Pilate's perspective. Would Jesus bring an army? How large would it be? Since He was said to be "King of the Jews" (Luke 23:3), would Jesus incite a rebellion among the Jews to usurp Pilate's position of authority? What sort of weaponry would He use? Pilate believed, as did many Jews of that day, that armed conflict alone could extend a kingdom. Since Jesus was a king, Pilate assumed He must command an army. This was the Roman way. The *Pax Romana* was maintained through force. Jesus' response to Pilate shows that Pilate failed to understand the nature of Jesus' kingdom.

Pilate tests Jesus by asking rhetorically, "So You are a king?" The accusation had been made by Jesus' enemies that He was a king, a political competitor to Pilate's throne. Jesus did not deny the claim even if Pilate did not understand its spiritual significance: "You say correctly that I am a king. For this I have been born, and for this I have come into the world, to bear witness to the truth. Every one who is of the truth hears My voice" (John 18:37). By this statement, Jesus made it clear that even Pilate was subject to God's government: "Jesus answered, 'You would have no authority over Me, unless it had been given you from above; for this reason he who delivered Me up to you has the greater sin'" (19:11). In fact, all who rule are subject to God's ultimate authority (Rom. 13:1), because Jesus is "ruler of the kings of the earth" (Rev. 1:5).

When Jesus kept silent regarding Pilate's question concerning His origin (John 19:9), Pilate grew indignant: "You do not speak to me? Do you not know that I have authority to release You, and I have authority to crucify You?" (19:10). Jesus' answer settled the matter about the operation of God's kingdom. Unless the kingdom of God operated *in* and *over* this world, what Jesus said next would carry no weight: "You would have no authority over Me, *unless it had been given you from above . . .*" (19:11).

Looking for Political Solutions

Confusion over Jesus' words develops from a false notion that the answer to man's problems is solely political. There were numerous occasions when the crowds wanted to make Him King (*e.g.*, John 6:15).

While there are political implications to Jesus' kingship, just as there are personal, familial, economic, business, ecclesiastical, and judicial implications, *the kingdom of God cannot be brought about politically*, either by the vote or violence. Good laws do not make good people. They can at best prepare people to become good people by *restraining outward evil* (1 Tim. 1:8–11). The law is a "tutor," an instructor to show us our sin and our need of redemption. (Gal. 3:24–25). Only the sovereign work of the Holy Spirit in regeneration makes people good. The State has a God-imposed jurisdiction to perform kingdom activities related to *civil* affairs according to the specifics of God's Word.

Many in Jesus' day saw the kingdom of God in externals only. They visualized the kingdom of God as coming, not through regeneration, but through social revolution. Jesus said of His followers: "Truly, truly, I say to you, you seek Me, not because you saw signs, but because you ate of the loaves, and were filled" (John 6:26). It was Jesus' message about mankind's need for salvation and about Him as the Savior, the Messiah of God, that caused the religious and political establishments of the day to seek His death.

The kingdom of God never advances through political intrigue, backed by military power. Though power-directed, its power comes from above and works on and in the heart of man: "I will give you a new heart and put a new spirit within you; and I will remove the heart of stone from your flesh and give you a heart of flesh. And I will put My Spirit within you and cause you to walk in My statutes, and you will be careful to observe My ordinances" (Ezek. 36:26–27). Self-government, wherein God subdues the heart to teachableness, leads to godly family, church, and civil governments (cf. 1 Tim. 1:8–11).

The supernatural power that energizes God's kingdom is never bound by political rhetoric: "For the kingdom of God does not consist in words, but in power" (1 Cor. 4:20). The battle against the kingdoms of this world is waged through the awesome power inherent in God's Word, energized by His Spirit: "For though we walk in the flesh, we do not war according to the flesh, for the weapons of our warfare are not of the flesh, but divinely powerful for the destruction of fortresses" (2 Cor.

10:3–4). As Christians, "we are destroying speculations and every lofty thing raised up against the knowledge of God, and we are taking every thought captive to the obedience of Christ" (2 Cor. 10:5). This is the nature of true kingdom living.

Saved by Law?

Old Testament Israel was given what can be described as a full-orbed or comprehensive biblical worldview. Every area of life was to be interpreted in terms of God's revealed law. The law was God's *standard* of righteousness; it was never designed to make a person righteous.

Too many Christians have been lead astray with the false notion that Israel was saved by the law (never its God-designed function) while New Testament believers are saved by grace through faith.[1] The false inference is made that since the law played such a major part in Israel's salvation and grace now plays the major part in the Christian's life, the law should be abandoned in favor of grace.

There is really no justification for such a belief. The Israelites were to have circumcised hearts, equivalent to the New Testament's requirement to be "born again" (John 3:3), both the work of God.

> • "Circumcise then your heart, and stiffen your neck no more" (Deut. 10:16)
> • "Moreover the LORD your God will circumcise your heart and the heart of your descendants, to love the LORD your God with all your heart and with all your soul, in order that you may live" (30:6).

This is regeneration. This is not justification through the works of the law. Regeneration makes the heart of stiff-necked and rebellious men and women submit willingly to their heavenly Father. When the heart is made new, it is able and ready to love. How do we show our love for God? By keeping His commandments. Isn't this what Deuteronomy 30:6 maintains? Isn't this what the New Testament tells us? (John 14:15).

Israel's keeping the law was an expression of their love for God, not a method to gain God's acceptance.

The proper ordering of society arises from regenerate individuals who move into the broader culture to be "salt and light" (Matt. 5:13–16). Salt is a preservative, keeping the culture from experiencing social entropy, the inevitable decline of society as sin works out its rotting effects. The Christian also is light, pointing out the way to the spiritually blind.

Many Christians contend that if enough people are saved, the broader culture will change automatically. On the surface this might seem reasonable. But it misses a vital element. While the regenerate person certainly has a new disposition to do right, he is often left without knowing what to do. The specific ethic of God's revealed laws has been reduced to the single ethic of "love." Of course, the Bible does command us to love, but love without specific guidelines is nothing more than sentimentality (Rom. 13:8–10).

The Earth Is the Lord's

Restoration begins by realizing that we live in the midst of God's kingdom. God's pattern for godly living is established in heaven. In the Lord's Prayer we petition God, "Thy Kingdom come. Thy will be done, on earth as it is in heaven" (Matt. 6:10). God has not called us to forsake the earth, but to impress heaven's pattern on earth.

Christians are to be in the world, but they are not to be of the world (John 12:26–27). They are not to be squeezed into the world's mold (Rom 12:2). They are not to be led astray by the "elementary principles of the world" (Col. 2:8). They are to keep themselves "unstained by the world" (James 1:27). They are warned not to get entangled in the "defilements of the world" (2 Peter 2:20). Nowhere are they told to abandon the world (Matt. 12:26–27).

The "world" is corrupt because people are corrupt. When corrupt people control certain aspects of the world, we can expect defilement. But the world does not have to remain in decay. When individuals are redeemed, the effects of their redemption should spread to the society in which they live and conduct their affairs.

The world of pagan thinking and practice is to be replaced by Christian thinking and practice. It is a perversion of the gospel to maintain that the world, as the domain where evil exists, is inherently corrupt. We should remember that Jesus came to this world to give His life for its redemption (John 3:16).

A Cleansed and Redeemed Earth

There is no inherent sinfulness in material things. Scripture says Jesus shared in "flesh and blood" (Heb. 2:14). He who denies that Jesus Christ has come in the flesh "is the deceiver and the antichrist" (2 John 7; cf. 1 John 4:1-3). Man's body is not inherently sinful. We shall have bodies in the resurrection, as Jesus does (John 12:26–27). In the resurrection, we will be "raised imperishable" (1 Cor. 15:52).

By denying the spirituality of God's created order, we neglect its importance and give it by default to those who deny Christ. *Worldliness* is to be avoided, not the world. God created everything wholly good (Gen. 1:31). Man, through the Fall, became profane and defiled by sin. Redemption restores all things in Christ.

Peter failed to understand the gospel's comprehensive cleansing effects. He could not believe the Gentiles were "clean": "What God has cleansed, no longer consider unholy" (Acts 10:15; Matt. 15:11; Rom. 14:14, 20). We should not say that the Fall eradicated God's pronouncement that the created order "was very good" (Gen. 1:31). The New Testament reinforces the goodness of God's creation: "For everything created by God is good, and nothing is to be rejected, if it is received with gratitude; for it is sanctified by means of the word of God and prayer" (1 Tim. 4:4–5).

The Bible: Not Silent on Politics

The Bible is filled with "politics." Here are just a few examples of political concerns found in the Bible: Noah is given authority to execute murderers (Gen. 9:6–7); Joseph is made ruler in Egypt (41:38–

49); "case laws" are tabulated for family, church, and State (Ex. 21–23); God instructs both priests and kings to follow the law of God (Deut.17:14–20); the book of Judges shows the interrelationship between religion and government; 1 Samuel 8 shows how rejecting God as Israel's true King leads to tyranny; the books of Samuel, Kings, and Chronicles tell of the rise and fall of kings and kingdoms, with individual kings singled out for special counsel by God's emissaries (*e.g.*, Jer. 36–38); Daniel serves as one of Darius' three civil commissioners (Dan. 6). The realm of "politics," or civil government, is given much attention in the Bible, in both the Old and New Testaments. Kenneth L. Gentry, Jr. writes:

> That God is vitally concerned with political affairs is quite easy to demonstrate: it is God who ordained governments in the first place (Rom. 13:1; Rom. 2:21). He is the One who establishes particular kings (Prov. 16:12; Psa. 119:46, 47; 82:1, 2). Therefore, He commands our obedience to rulers (Rom. 13:1–3). Rulers are commanded to rule on His terms (Psa. 2:10ff.). Even in the New Testament activity of political import is discoverable. Jesus urged payment of taxes to *de facto* governments (Matt. 22:15–22). In response to reminders of King Herod's political threats against Him, Jesus publicly rebuked the king by calling him a vixen (Luke 12:32). He taught that a judge is unjust if he does not fear God (Luke 18:2, 6). John the Baptist openly criticized King Herod (Luke 3:19, 20). Peter refused to obey authorities who commanded him to cease preaching (Acts 5:29). The Apostle John referred to the Roman Empire as "the beast" (Rev. 13).[2]

Denial of political involvement repudiates much of the Bible. Paul makes it clear that the "saints will judge the world" (1 Cor. 6:2). The context of this verse has to do with constituting "the smallest law courts." Christians at various times in history have "judged the world." The foundation of Western legal tradition is Christian. The demise of the

West results from Christians' non-involvement in every sphere of life, the civil sphere included.

Legislating Either Morality or Immorality

Life's political sphere should not be used to change or reform men and women (though the fear of punishment does change people from considering criminal activity). The law's purpose as it relates to the civil magistrate is to punish and restrain evil, to protect human life and property, and to provide justice for all people, using God's Word as the standard. Only God can regenerate the heart. An individual cannot be made good by law-keeping.

The Bible exists as the State's perfect standard of justice. In fact, this truth remains primary in the establishment of justice. When the Bible speaks to *civil* affairs, *civil* government has a duty to heed its commands. How will civil government determine what is good or evil, unless God's law is consulted? Where God's law is not the standard, there can be no objective standard for man to follow.

We live in an era in which the Bible is rejected as the State's authority. Killing unborn babies is legal, and the State, through a corrupt tax system, uses the tax money to support this heinous crime. Religion, and in particular, biblical law, cannot be separated from life in general and politics in particular.

For example, during the time of fuel shortages when OPEC cut oil production, the speed limit in the United States was reduced from 70 mph to 55 mph for two advertised reasons. First, to save lives. Second, to cut fuel consumption. Both reasons are value-laden and rest on moral considerations. They presuppose that human life is valuable and that society at large is valuable (if the world runs out of fuel, then everyone is hurt). Laws were instituted to enforce these moral, value-laden concerns.

Dirty Politics?

Things in themselves are not sinful. The "tree of the knowledge of good and evil" (Gen. 2:16) was not evil. Even as Adam and Eve ate the fruit, the fruit was not evil. The Garden where they committed their sin was not evil. The decision they made was sinful. What they did with God's good creation was sinful.

The political sphere is a created entity. So is the family and church. Anyone who would say that *on principle* he wants nothing to do with either church government or family government is clearly a covenant-breaker. The same is true of anyone who says that on principle he wants nothing to do with civil government.

Mankind images God. God is the Governor over all creation; He has called us to be governors under His one government. The civil sphere is an area of legitimate governmental activity. Politics is "dirty" when men and women break God's law. So is every other area of human responsibility: business, law, education, labor, sports, or whatever. Sin has affected every institution. This means that *God's law has called every institution into judgment.* In short, *no law–no sin* (Rom. 7:7–12). The person who says that God's law does not judge every area of life and every institution is saying that these institutions are immune from the effects of sin. But they *are* dirty because sinners are involved. Christians therefore must insist that the gospel of Jesus Christ can cleanse every institution from sin, because institutions are run by fallen people. God has given us a *comprehensive gospel* that offers *comprehensive redemption.*

Christians should be involved in politics because it's dirty. Who else has the means to clean it (or any other area of human activity)? If Christians do not, who will? Christians have stayed out of politics, making its corruption even more pronounced. The answer is not to consign politics to more corruption by ignoring it as an area for redemption and restoration.

The Bible never condemns political involvement. John the Baptist does not rebuke Herod for his political position, but for his sinful actions as a governor. Jesus does not quarrel with Pontius Pilate over whether he should rule, but only reminds him *why* he rules and, implicitly, by what standard he rules. Paul calls rulers God's "ministers," servants in the political sphere (Rom. 13:4). Paul used his Roman citizenship when it was appropriate (Acts 22:28). Paul appeals to Caesar, the seat of Roman *political* power, in order to gain a hearing (25:11).

The desire to retreat from political concerns is recent within our history. John Witherspoon, a minister in the Presbyterian church and the President of the College of New Jersey (which later became Princeton), signed the Declaration of Independence. The framers of the Constitution, "with no more than five exceptions (and perhaps no more than three), . . . were orthodox members of one of the established Christian communions: approximately twenty-nine Anglicans, sixteen to eighteen Calvinists, two Methodists, two Lutherans, two Roman Catholics, one lapsed Quaker and sometime-Anglican, and one open Deist Dr. [Benjamin] Franklin, who attended every kind of Christian worship, called for public prayer, and contributed to all denominations."[3] It was Franklin who declared to the members of the Constitutional Convention, quoting the Bible, "Unless the Lord builds the house, they labor in vain who build it" (Psalm 127:1). He went on to state that their efforts would be no better than the builders of Babel if they forgot who ultimately rules in the affairs of men, including political affairs.

Summary Concepts

For many Christians, evil times are sure evidence that the end is near, and Jesus is about to return to remove us from a steadily decaying world. Such "prophetic pronouncements" have become self-fulfilling. For generations, Christians have been saying, "This is it! Now is the time for the end!" They all have one thing in common: They've all been wrong![4] Instead of Christians working out their salvation with fear and trembling, the church of Jesus Christ has retreated into passivity in fear and trembling.

In the process of retreatism, in the face of an advancing secularism, things have gotten worse. But what do we expect? We've removed the only preserving factor, the church of Jesus Christ, as the salt of the earth. Things will be even worse for the next generation. What will these Christians do? Will they also maintain that it's the end? Or will they see the errors of the past and work to preserve and reform the world to the glory of God and the advancement of the Christian faith through the preaching of the gospel and the discipleship of the nations?

Christians ought to be turning the world "right side up" through the preaching of the gospel and the application of God's law to every area of life. This is all possible because Jesus' kingdom operates in the world although it does not derive its sovereignty, authority, and power from this world.

Jesus was a threat to the religious and political leaders of His day because He held them accountable to His law. On the other hand, others looked to Jesus as a political messiah, rejecting His saving work and the demand for repentance.

The earth belongs to the Lord and to those whom He gives it as an inheritance. The world has been cleansed by the blood of Christ; therefore, let us not call unholy what God now calls holy. God ordained government. Government, even civil government, is good. The Bible is filled with politics. For example, there are two books in the Bible titled "Kings."

Politics is not inherently sinful. Politicians may be, but so are fathers, mothers, children, teachers, businessmen, ministers, and doctors. God calls His people to act out the redemption Jesus has accomplished for the whole universe. Remember, Jesus is the Savior of the *world*.

Summary Principles

1. No man can serve two masters.
2. We need to serve a righteous master who gives us righteous law, and who judges righteously.
3. The Bible must provide our definition of "righteous."
4. The issue therefore is ethics.
5. The fundamental issues of government are ethical issues.
6. A law says yes to one group and no to another.
7. In the early church, the issue was: Christ or Caesar?
8. The humanists of the Roman Empire were threatened by the church.

9. That first-century world-transforming Christian faith has not been brought into this century.

10. Jesus' kingdom did not originate in this world, but it was always intended to change this world.

11. The kingdom of God cannot be brought in politically.

12. The people followed Jesus because He fed them by the miracle of the loaves.

13. The kingdom of God is powerful: the power of the Spirit.

14. A war is in progress between Christ's kingdom and the kingdoms of this world.

15. We are to pray that God's kingdom impresses itself on the institutions of this world.

16. The world can be progressively molded by Christ's kingdom.

17. The world can become cleansed progressively.

18. The Bible does establish guidelines for politics, although it is not a political book.

19. The denial of political involvement is the denial of many portions of the Bible.

20. Law legislates either morality or immorality.

21. There is no such thing as neutral legislation.

22. Religion and politics are already mixed.

23. The question is: Which religion?

24. Politics is dirty because Christians have abandoned politics.

25. God's law has called every institution under judgment.

Notes

1. When Paul sets forth the doctrine of justification by grace through faith in the letter to the Romans, he uses Old Testament examples, Abraham (before the giving of the law) and David (after the giving of the law) (Rom. 4).

2. Kenneth L. Gentry, Jr., "The Greatness of the Great Commission," *Journal of Christian Reconstruction*, Symposium on Evangelism, 7:2 (Winter 1981), 45.

3. M. E. Bradford, *A Worthy Company* (Marlborough, NH: Plymouth Rock Foundation, 1982), viii.

4. Francis X. Gumerlock, *The Day and the Hour: Christianity's Perennial Fascination with Predicting the End of the World* (Powder Springs, GA: American Vision, 2000).

Judges Need Jurisdiction

Let every person be in subjection to the governing authorities. For there
is no authority except from God, and those which exist are established
by God (Rom. 13:1).

The frame of reference in Romans 13 is civil, but not exclusively so.
God has established authorities: multiple civil jurisdictions as well as
authority in general. We are all under some authority. This is a fundamental aspect of biblical government. Power is not to be concentrated
in any single office.

The most important division is between the office of king and
priest. The power of one office is to be augmented by the other, and to
be checked and balanced to curtail the rise of tyranny. Both are offices
under God. Both represent God in their limited spheres of jurisdiction.

When judgment is brought in God's name, it must be within a
lawfully designated jurisdiction. Churches do not physically punish law-
breakers, and civil governments do not excommunicate church members and deny them access to the Lord's Supper. Civil governments do
not possess the authority to turn people over to Satan in order that they
might be brought back inside the covenant (1 Cor. 5:5).

Because so many people today do not fear God or God's eternal judgment, they do not fear excommunication. Churches that do not honor (at least by a careful investigation of the facts and trial) the excommunications of other churches are adding their authority to the skepticism of the covenant-breakers. So what do men fear today? They fear an institution that can punish them physically and economically: the State. As men lose faith in God, they gain new respect for the State. This is a great temptation for officers of civil governments to usurp their God-given authority and extend their jurisdiction beyond what God has delegated. But judgment eventually comes. In the Old Testament, it sometimes came in the most feared form of all: *leprosy*.

Leprosy and Jurisdiction

Leprosy! The word strikes terror in those who know its disfiguring work. We are not sure that the disease we call leprosy today is the same as the one called leprosy in the Bible. Even so, it was a horrible disease. Lepers were placed under quarantine (Lev. 13), isolated from family, work, and worship. It was considered the ultimate curse. Victims were not merely sick; they were "unclean." Leprosy was like sin; its infection would slowly consume its host. There was no known cure other than divine intervention. *It was considered the special judgment of God, and only God could remove it.* This is one reason why anyone cured of leprosy had to offer special sacrifices to make atonement (Lev. 14).

When we raise the subject of leprosy, we raise the subject of lawful jurisdiction (law=*juris*; declare=*dictio*). In the Old Testament, the priests had jurisdiction over quarantine for leprosy. They would declare a suspected person either leprous or clean. Their word was sovereign.

Miriam

Miriam, Moses' sister, was struck with leprosy when she and Aaron challenged God's choice of Moses as His mediator. "So the anger of the LORD burned against them [Miriam and Aaron] and He departed. But when the cloud had withdrawn from over the tent, behold, Miriam was leprous, as white as snow. As Aaron turned toward Miriam, behold, she was leprous" (Num. 12:10). Their challenge was a serious offense. Aaron was the high priest, the supreme religious leader in Israel. Miriam was a prophetess and head of the spirit-filled women (Ex. 15:20–21). Though they each held high *religious* positions in Israel, their authority was limited by God. Any attempt to usurp the mediatorial position given to Moses by God was met with judgment.

Uzziah

God's laws are not to be tampered with. King Uzziah is said to have been "proud" (2 Chron. 26:16). His pride lead him to go beyond his jurisdiction. While he was "chief of State," being the king in Judah, he was not a priest. King Uzziah could not assume the role of a priest and perform ecclesiastical functions. He had no jurisdiction in the Temple, the Old Testament equivalent of the New Testament Church. Uzziah ignored God's law and "acted corruptly, and he was unfaithful to the LORD his God, for he entered the temple of the LORD to burn incense on the altar of incense" (2 Chron. 26:16).

Is God serious about this jurisdictional separation? Apparently He is. The king was struck with leprosy! "And king Uzziah was a leper to the day of his death; and he lived in a separate house, being a leper, for he was cut off from the house of the LORD" (26:21). He lost access to the Temple, was isolated from the general population, and lost his kingdom to his son, Jotham, who "was over the king's house judging the people of the land" (26:21).

The Priests

Azariah the priest was not passive in this whole affair. He knew the limitations of the king's power. He, along with "eighty priests of the LORD" (2 Chron. 26:17), took action against the king. Notice that they "opposed Uzziah the king" (26:18). They informed him that "it is not for you, Uzziah, to burn incense to the LORD, but for the priests, the sons of Aaron who are consecrated to burn incense" (26:18). The priests commanded Uzziah to "get out of the sanctuary" (26:18).

These "ecclesiastical officials" are called "valiant men" (26:17). Why? They acted with great risk. While there were eighty of them, the King still commanded an army. He could have put them to death. There was a precedent for this, when Ahimelech the priest helped David against King Saul (1 Sam. 21–22). King Saul called on Doeg the Edomite to attack the priests, after the King's own servants refused. "And Doeg the Edomite turned around and attacked the priests, and he killed that day eighty-five who wore the linen ephod" (22:18). Doeg the Edomite, one who despised the covenant, had no qualms about killing the priests. King Uzziah had Saul's hate in his eye: "Uzziah, with a censer in his hand for burning incense, was enraged" (2 Chron. 26:19) when confronted by the priests.

The priests were not casual about their duties. Too often the church has been passive as the State has increasingly encroached on the jurisdiction of the Church. While the priests of the temple knew their lives were at stake, they were more concerned with the "honor of the LORD" (26:18).

The Limits of Jurisdiction

While the Bible defines the *limits* of jurisdiction, it must also be used to prescribe the *specifics of operation* for each jurisdiction. The Bible is a blueprint for family government, for church government, and for civil government. If the Bible is the blueprint for only the family and Church and not the State, then immediate jurisdictional infringements take place. For example, according to the Bible, parents have educational jurisdiction of their children. If the State repudiates the Bible as a blueprint for Statecraft, children will be seen as wards of the State and come under its jurisdiction. Taxes will be raised by the State, teachers will be certified by the State, schools will be accredited by the State, and students will be compelled by the State to be educated by the State.

What if the State decides that more taxes are needed to fund some of its programs (programs that must be defined by the Bible)? Can the

State legitimately tax the church to raise the needed revenue? The State certainly has the authority and power to tax (Rom. 13:7; Matt. 22:15–22). But can it tax any way and in any amount it wishes? Can it tax the church? If the Bible is not a blueprint for taxation and the limits of civil jurisdiction, then the State is free to tax as it pleases.

God has established both church and State. They are not, in principle, hostile toward one another. But because each is a government, with a certain amount of authority and power, we should expect power struggles. Sometimes the power struggle is the Church attempting to impose its will on the State or using the power of the State to extend what is essentially a spiritual kingdom. This is not true church growth.

Church/State Cooperation

The Bible portrays Church and State as cooperating governments. Most people are aware that the Bible is the standard for the priests as they carry out their priestly duties. But what of the king? Was he obligated to follow the Bible as well? The Bible makes it clear that he was:

> Now it shall come about when he [the king] sits on the throne of his kingdom, he shall write for himself a copy of this law on a scroll in the presence of the Levitical priests. And it shall be with him, and he shall read it all the days of his life, that he may learn to fear the LORD his God, by carefully observing all the words of this law and these statutes, that his heart may not be lifted up above his countrymen and that he may not turn aside from the commandment, to the right or the left; in order that he and his sons may continue to live long in his kingdom in the midst of Israel (Deut. 17:18–20).

While Church and State as *jurisdictions* are separate, religion is not. Both priests and kings are commanded to follow the same standard of government, even though not all laws apply to each in the same way. We can go so far as to say that the presence of the priests served as a reminder to the king that they were to help him interpret the law as it related to civil affairs. This is precisely what Azariah and the eighty priests were doing when they confronted King Uzziah: They were reminding him of his limited jurisdiction.

Moral Criteria for Rulership

The criteria for leadership in both Church and State is the same. When Jethro, Moses' father-in-law, counseled Moses to decentralize the judicial arm of the civil government and choose lesser magistrates, he laid down the qualifications for those who would rule. They were to be "able men who fear God, men of truth, those who hate dishonest gain" (Ex. 18:21). Later, Moses recounts the circumstances of Jethro's counsel and adds that these leaders were to be "wise and discerning and experienced men," not showing "partiality in judgment" (Deut. 1:13, 17).

Church leaders in the New Testament are to exhibit similar ethical qualities and real life experience (1 Tim. 3:1–7). Being "above reproach" can be compared to "men of truth." "Those who hate dishonest gain" is similar to being "free from the love of money." An "experienced" man is someone who is "not a new convert."

Parallel Jurisdictions

Moses became the chief judicial officer in Israel, assisted by numerous lesser magistrates (Ex. 18:17–26). Aaron, Moses' brother, became the chief ecclesiastical officer as High Priest, assisted by numerous lesser priests (Lev. 8).

In the days of the Judges, Othniel, Ehud, Shamgar, Gideon and Samson served as political officers (Judges 1–13), while the son of Micah, Phineas, Eli, and the Levites served in an ecclesiastical capacity (Judges 17; 20:28; 1 Sam. 1–8).

During the period of the monarchy, King Saul served in a civil capacity while Ahimelech ministered as the chief ecclesiastical leader in the nation (1 Sam. 10 and 21). There was King David and Priest Abiathar

(1 Chron. 15:11), King Solomon and Priest Zadok (1 Kings 1:45), King Joash and Priest Jehoiada (2 Kings 11), and King Josiah and Priest Hilkiah (2 Kings 22:4).

Even after the return from exile, Church and State as parallel institutions operated with Governor Nehemiah (Neh. 7) and Priest Ezra (Neh. 8). This jurisdictional cooperation culminated in the priestly office of Joshua and the civil office of Zerubbabel (Zech. 4:14).

All Are Ministers

The New Testament describes leaders in the Church and State as "ministers" (Mark 10:42–45 and Rom. 13:4). Even when describing the role of the civil magistrate, the Greek word for "deacon" is used.

The Greek words used for "minister" and "deacon" underscore the ruler's duty to *serve* rather than to "lord it over" those under his authority. Truly and lasting dominion comes through service. The civil "minister" rules for our "good," and he is "an avenger who brings wrath upon the one who practices evil" (Rom. 13:4). How does the civil magistrate determine what is "good" from what is "evil"? As God's "minister," he must consult God's Word.

Jurisdictional Usurpation

There is always the danger of Jurisdictional usurpation; for example, when civil government removes the Jurisdictional framework of the church. The Bible cites a number of examples of how the king sought to overrule the authority and function of the church. King Saul assumed for himself the duties of the priests when he offered sacrifices rather than staying within the bounds of his kingly duties (1 Sam. 15:9–15, 22). In another place, King Saul killed the godly priest Ahimelech because he would not fulfill the king's political goals (21:1).

King Jeroboam established his State religion in Bethel and Dan. Non-Levites of the worst character were appointed to serve as priests (1 Kings 12:26–31). Of course, we've already seen how King Uzziah was struck with leprosy for usurping the priestly function of burning incense in the temple (2 Chron. 26:16).

But there are times when the church forgets its God-ordained role. The church can deny its prophetic ministry when it is seduced by politics, having lost faith in our Transcendent God, putting trust in human action. Isn't this what happened when the people wanted to crown Jesus as King, to make Him their political ruler? They had given up hope in the transformation of man from the inside out. They denied the transforming work of the Holy Spirit to regenerate the dead heart of man. Man's salvation would come through political power. Jesus rebuffed their desires to make Him a political savior. While politics has a role to play, it is only one role among many.

Summary Concepts

The ninth basic principle in the Biblical blueprint for civil government is that lawful jurisdiction for any government is established by God in the Bible. To violate these God-ordained jurisdictions is to become rebellious. It brings on God's judgment in history.

God judges those who tamper with His law. There is a *jurisdictional* separation between church and State. The Bible defines the limits of jurisdiction. Church and State were established to cooperate, not compete. Leadership in both church and State is based on *ethical* considerations. Church and State are *parallel* governments bound by the same law. Leaders in both Church and State are given the title "minister." The Bible condemns jurisdictional usurpation.

God establishes multiple government jurisdictions, and therefore multiple hierarchies, in order to reflect His own plural nature, but also to restrain the sinfulness of man. He brought judgment in history against the builders of the Tower of Babel because they proposed to build a one-world messianic State. They wanted to give their own name to themselves, defining themselves without reference to God, and to establish their own jurisdictions.

The criteria for serving as a judge, in church and State, is morality.

Men are not to use their offices to pursue personal economic gain or power. They are to execute judgment as God's delegated representatives. This representative character of all civil and ecclesiastical offices is basic to every human government.

God brings His people freedom. One means to this freedom is a system of potentially competing delegated sovereignties. When men sin, and overstep their limits (the meaning of sin), they often try to extend their authority over others. Parallel governments help to reduce the extent of such lawless behavior with checks and balances.

Most Americans are confused when it comes to church/State relations. If they were asked to choose between the language of the First Amendment of our Constitution and the language of the Soviet Constitution, few could tell the difference. The critics of Christ and His law have done a masterful job in rewriting history.

Summary Principles

1. All authority is delegated from God.
2. Obedience to God-authorized judges is required.
3. There is no single human authority; human authority is always plural.
4. King and priest are the most obvious examples of divided authority.
5. When judgment is brought in God's name, it must be within a lawfully designated jurisdiction.
6. Men mainly fear the State today because they do not fear God or excommunication.
7. Leprosy was an Old Testament judgment from God.
8. King Uzziah was judged with leprosy because he refused to honor the jurisdictional separation of the sanctuary.
9. The secular humanist State refuses to honor the other jurisdictions: family and church.
10. Fathers possess God-given limited authority over wives and children.

11. The church is the primary protector of the family.

12. The family is not "the key" institution; the church is.

13. The church's weapons are preaching, the sacraments, and prayer (for example, imprecatory psalms).

14. The Bible establishes the jurisdictional limits on each institution.

15. Church and State should cooperate.

16. Both are under Biblical law; both must rule (judge) in terms of Biblical law.

17. The criteria are moral for both the civil and ecclesiastical offices.

18. The jurisdictions are parallel.

19. The officers of both are ministers of God.

Rebuilding Takes Time

For who has despised the day of small things? (Zech. 4:10).

Depression can easily set in when you consider how far behind Christians are compared to where they were two hundred years ago in terms of cultural and moral impact and influence on society. There was a time when civilization was defined in terms of a Christian worldview. Music, art, literature, journalism, education, and even science had a Christian foundation.[1] We have a lot of lost ground to recover. For example:

- Hardcore humanists dominate broadcast television. This includes CBS, NBC, ABC, MSNBC, and CNN news broadcasts and nearly all television entertainment. FOX is an exception, but it's the exception that proves the rule.
- Liberals dominate education at all levels: Conservative college professors are outnumbered by liberals twenty to one. Campus newspapers and the implementation of "speech codes" are led by secularists who want free speech for them but restricted speech for opposing opinions. Law schools, medical schools, and schools of education, which supply training for our nation's public school

teachers, are dominated by liberals.

• Liberals dominate Hollywood: Political activists are almost all pro-abortion, pro-homosexual, pro-big-government liberals. With few exceptions, movies often depict clergy in a negative way.

• Liberals govern the biggest foundations, such as the Pew Memorial Trust and the Ford and Rockefeller Foundations, to fund leftist political causes.

• Liberals dominate almost every major newspaper both in news coverage and editorial opinion: While there are exceptions, such as the *Wall Street Journal* and *Washington Times*, the papers most often cited in news reports by other liberal papers and news sources are from liberal newspapers like the *Boston Globe*, the *New York Times*, the *Washington Post*, *USA Today*, the *Los Angeles Times*, the *Miami Herald*, and the *Chicago Tribune*.

• Liberals dominate the weekly news magazines: With circulation in the millions, *Time*, *U.S. News & World Report*, and *Newsweek* present a consistent liberal slant in their news coverage. When they do cover a religious topic, they most often lean left in the sources they cite.

• Liberals dominate virtually every professional organization: the American Bar Association, American Psychiatric Association, American Library Association, American Nurses Association, National Education Association, American Political Science Association, the Trial Lawyers Association and every big labor union.

• Liberals dominate much of organized religion: the mainstream Protestant churches and Reform and Conservative Judaism; while the liberal social message (with the exception of abortion rights) dominates much of the Roman Catholic Church.

• Liberals dominate activist groups: National Organization for Women (NOW), National Association for the Advancement of Colored People (NAACP), the American Civil Liberties Union (ACLU), as well as the National Abortion Rights Action League

(NARAL), and prominent homosexual groups that bully legislators, school boards, and private organizations like the Boy Scouts to accept their immoral lifestyle.[2]

These facts could depress even the most optimistic Christian. We have lost a tremendous amount of ground over the last two centuries. It's going to take a long time to make it up. The only events that might speed up this timetable would be a massive revival of self-government under God—or a terrible catastrophe: a lost war, a plague, or both. In either case, Christians will be called upon to exercise responsibility under God as never before. But how will they train themselves in advance to exercise such responsibility in a culture that promises continued benefits without revival? What if they are not prepared to take responsibility? *How do you sell responsibility to modern Christians?*

What if a group of dedicated Christians were to buy one of our nations most prominent newspaper? What difference would it make? Not much. Where would the owners find the reporters who understand biblical principles, and who will write the articles from a biblical perspective? Would the editor even be willing to risk dropping the daily astrology column? Without a legion of dedicated, well-trained, biblically self-conscious professionals, the ownership of a newspaper (or television network, or anything else) would not mean very much. In fact, it would probably mean financial losses as the new owners floundered with the responsibilities of management and inexperience.

Double Your Pleasure

We have a big job ahead of us. But what should encourage every Christian is the truth of Zechariah 4:10. Beginning to do something, even if it's a small thing, is the main thing. Consider this question: If a piece of paper could be folded in half just fifty times, with the doubling of pages on every fold, how thick would it be? On the first fold there would be 2 pieces of paper, then 4 on the next fold, then 8, then 16, 32, 64, 128, 256, 512, 1012, 2,024, 4,048, etc. until fifty doublings were reached. This would give you 1,125,800,000,000,000 sheets of paper. Divide this number by 200, the number of sheets of paper needed to make an inch, and you wind up with 5,629,400,000,000 inches. Divide this by 12, the number of inches in a foot, and you get 469,120,000,000 feet. This number is then divided by 5280, the number of feet in a mile, with 88,849,424 miles as the result, nearly the distance from the earth to the sun. Therefore, if a piece of paper could be folded in half just fifty times, it would be nearly as tall as the distance from the earth to the sun. Don't believe me? Try it yourself by beginning with 2^{50} and then following the steps outlined above.[3]

What's the point of the math lesson? Too often we discount our seemingly meager efforts to transform society as being too little to make any lasting difference. We may hear of a small reformation taking place in the northwest and in a few cities in the south, but this does little to impress us when we see liberalism everywhere. Like the person who begins to play the guitar and stops when it proves a little difficult, we stop our goal of reformation when we don't see immediate exponential growth. We then convince ourselves that it's not in God's plan to bring about worldwide reformation.

Consider what's going to happen in the not too distant future if homeschooling and the broader Christian school movement increase at their present rates. They will, by mathematical formulation, reach a tipping point where, seemingly, almost overnight, societal change has occurred. These graduates will demand a different kind of higher education or no institutional higher education of any kind. As word gets out of its availability and quality, growth skyrockets. Like a flu epidemic, liberalism runs out of available converts. Christianity supplants the once-prevailing anti-Christian worldview. It all begins with a single fold of paper, or as Zechariah puts it, "For who has despised the day of small things?" (Zech. 4:10).

Being big enough to do something is never an issue in the Bible. The giants did not seem to bother Joshua and Caleb; Goliath was no problem for David; and faith the size of a mustard seed is all the Christian needs to move a mountain.

Civilizations come and go, but the kingdom of God goes on forever. This is the point of Nebuchadnezzar's dream of the human colossus. Kingdoms built on the shaky foundation that man is sovereign cannot last. Pick up any history book, and you can read about the demise of every empire-building civilization. They are dust on the cosmic scales of God's justice.

Christians have lost sight of the stone cut without hands that became a mountain that filled the earth (Dan. 2:35). For some reason we just cannot seem to believe that Jesus, through His redeemed people, is the fulfillment of that prophecy (cf. 1 Peter 2:5). We have convinced ourselves that defeat is the only option for the church. The only hope is retreat in the face of a creeping secularism. Maybe if things get real bad God will rapture us out of this mess.[4]

Unbelief and Defeat

It is interesting to note that every time there was any consideration of retreat in the face of opposition, the people of God were rebuked for their unbelief. For example, when the 12 spies were sent out to Canaan, God had promised them that the land would be theirs: "Send out for yourself men so that they may spy out the land of Canaan, *that I am going to give to the sons of Israel*" (Num. 13:2).

You know the story: Ten of the spies came back with a report steeped in unbelief. Joshua and Caleb believed God. Sure, there were giants in the land. Joshua and Caleb never denied this. So what? God is the Lord. The promise was made, the land was theirs. Giants are nothing more than a minor and temporary inconvenience.

Forty years were wasted in the wilderness because the people chose to believe the report of the unbelieving spies. The giants turned out to be whimpering dogs. When two spies were sent out to Jericho forty years later, Rahab told the real story:

> I know that the LORD has given this land to you and that a
> great fear of you has fallen on us, so that all who live in this

country are melting in fear because of you. We have heard how
the LORD dried up the water of the Red Sea for you when you
came out of Egypt, and what you did to Sihon and Og, the two
kings of the Amorites east of the Jordan, whom you completely
destroyed. *When we heard of it, our hearts sank and everyone's
courage failed because of you, for the* LORD *your God is God in*
heaven above and on the earth beneath (Josh. 2:8–11).

There is little difference between the humanists of Rahab's day
and the humanists of our day. They are just as frightened as the residents of Jericho were. But today's Christians are unwilling to believe
this, any more than Joshua's generation was willing to believe it. And so
Christians have sat on the sidelines of life, waiting for God to bail them
out. Do you remember what God did to Joshua's generation? He did
not bail them out. He waited for them to die, and then He allowed
Joshua and Caleb to lead the next generation to victory (Num. 14:21–
23; Josh. 15:13–19).

Why Christians Should Get Involved

The people in Gideon's day saw politics alone as the solution to
their problems (Judges 8:22–23). If they just had a powerful king to
rule over them, their problems would be solved. When Abimelech murdered his opposition (9:1–6), he promised the people security if they
would only follow him. While there is the offer of shade (salvation), it is
an illusion that brings with it a choking tyranny (9:15).

When the lack of personal holiness corrupted the family (Judges
14–16) and priesthood (1 Sam. 2:12–17, 22–36), the people turned to
the State for salvation (1 Sam. 8). The Christian calls politics into question, not because it is an illegitimate sphere of Christian activity, but
because it is too often seen by people as the first road to restoration.
Politics was never meant to save mankind, and it cannot save. While
Christians are to redeem ("buy back") politics and the civil sphere of
government, we are never to view political action as the sole solution to

all our problems, or even the main solution.

The purpose of Christians' involvement in politics ought to be more than the mere replacement of non-Christians with Christians. A civil government based on biblical law would mean a drastic reduction in the size and power of the State and a return of jurisdictional authority to individuals, private enterprise, families, churches, and local civil governments.

The church has awakened (at least some of the church has) to her responsibilities in the area of worldview thinking. Christians are beginning to realize that the Bible has answers, that the Bible addresses the world with specific solutions to perplexing problems.

There are many Christians and non-Christians who do not like to think of the Bible in these terms. In fact, many are horrified at any suggestion that the world is in any way redeemable. They are content to ignore verses like "God so loved the world" (John 3:16); "God was in Christ reconciling the world to Himself" (2 Cor. 5:19); Jesus is "the light of the world" (John 8:12), "the Savior of the world" (4:42), and "the Lamb of God who takes away the sins of the world!" (1:29). And how about this one?: "the kingdom of the world *has become* the kingdom of our Lord, and of His Christ; and He will reign forever and ever" (Rev. 11:15).

Now, don't get me wrong. To say that the world is redeemed is not to say that the world can be made perfect. For example, the dead sinner is redeemed, but he is not perfect. Judicially, the sinner stands before God as perfect because he has the perfect righteousness of Christ *imputed* to him. He is not made righteous; he is declared righteous. This, however, does not exempt him from conforming his life more and more to the image of Jesus Christ. This process is called sanctification.

God expects the redeemed sinner to conform his behavior to the commandments of God, though the effects of his sin nature will not be eradicated until he is raised "imperishable" (1 Cor. 15:42). The implications of such a life are evident. If the redeemed sinner can change his life through sanctification, then how can we deny that the world is destined for corruption? Isn't the redeemed sinner both salt and light in the world? Let's face it, wherever the gospel has changed individuals it has changed civilizations. Just compare the Christian West with the paganism and cultural decline of other nations.

But what about the advance of humanism? The answer is quite simple: the *advance of humanism* is the result of the *retreat of Christianity*. Just as a neglected garden will be overwhelmed by weeds, so a neglected area of responsibility will be overwhelmed by evil.

Does Satan Have More Power Than Christians?

But what about the rise of demonic activity in our day? Many Christians point to this and say that this is proof that we're coming to the end of the world, meaning the end of the "Church Age." But there was also heightened demonic activity during Jesus' public ministry. Was this the end of the world? Yes! But not the end of the *Christian* world; it was the end of demon-sponsored humanism, Pharisaism, legalism, and Romanism. The pagans better understood the implications of Christianity than do many modern critics of civilization building: "These men who have upset the world have come here also" (Acts 17:6).

Gary North's analysis of occultism and New Age Humanism shows that "the rise of occultism takes place at the end of civilizations. . . . This humanist civilization has spent spiritual capital, and its checks are bouncing. The decay of humanism has led to the revival of occultism. What we are witnessing is *occult revival and cultural disintegration*. What we may very well be witnessing is *humanist civilization's dying gasp*."[5]

The collapse of humanism and the stench of occultism bring with them certain opportunities for Christians. The world is looking for answers. Christians, if they truly believe the Bible, have answers. Setting the agenda for the twenty-first century and beyond should be the priority for all Christians. This will mean involvement.

We are too often occupied with what man has done, all the while denying what God is doing. The way Christians think and act, one would suppose that Satan is more powerful than God. Satan has power, but it is limited by God. Even in the Old Testament era, Satan was restricted in the influence he could exert. Before Satan could afflict Job he had to seek God's permission: "Behold, all that he [Job] has is in your power, only do not put forth your hand on him" (Job 1:12; cf, 2:6). Through it all God received the glory and Job was finally restored (42:10–17).

During Jesus' earthly ministry, the disciples had authority and power over demons because Satan's power was partially grounded. When the seventy disciples returned from their mission they remarked that "even the demons are subject to us" (Luke 10:17). How could this be? "And He said to them, 'I was watching Satan fall from heaven like lightning. Behold, I have given you authority to tread upon serpents and scorpions, and over all the power of the enemy, and nothing shall injure you'" (10:17–18).

Jesus tells the Pharisees that His casting out demons is the sign that the kingdom of God has come, displacing the enemy territory of Satan: "But if I cast out demons by the finger of God, then the kingdom of God has come upon you. When a strong man [Satan] fully armed, guards his own household, his possessions are undisturbed; but when someone stronger [God] than he attacks him and overpowers him, he takes away from him all his armor on that he had relied, and distributes his plunder [Satan's kingdom]" (11:10–22).

When Jesus was about to go to the cross He made reference to the effect that Satan will have on His work: "I will not speak much more with you, for the ruler of the world is coming, and he has nothing in Me" (John 14:30). All the powers of Hell would not be able to deter Jesus in the task that would soon energize the church to such an extent that the gates of Hell will not be able to stand against her power: "Upon this rock [the sure testimony that Jesus is the Christ, the Son of the living God] I will build My church; and the gates of Hades shall not overpower it" (Matt. 16:18).

The apostle Paul, aware of the power of Rome and that many Christians would suffer at the hands of the State, strengthened them with these words: "And the God of peace will soon crush Satan under your feet" (Rom. 16:20). These Roman Christians could expect this "soon" by praying for it and carrying out their dominion task in every area of life. The Christian is able to spoil the works of the devil because of the limited power that Satan has over believers. He cannot "touch" a Christian (1 John 5:18); his works have been destroyed (1 John 3:8); he must flee when resisted (James 4:7); and he has been rendered power-less over believers (Heb. 2:14).

The above Scriptural evidence is of no use if Christians assume incorrectly that Satan is now in control, and that his controlling influence will continue. Of course, if Christians do nothing we can expect Satan's kingdom to advance. The whole world lies in the power of the evil one (1 John 5:19) as long as Christians refuse to plant and water the seeds of the gospel in the world. The power of Satan over the world is temporary until the nations are discipled (cf. Matt. 28:18–20). More-over, to say that Satan is in control of the governments of the world is to say that Christians have been irresponsible in transforming the civil realms of power according to the commandments of God. Christians have no excuse because God has "disarmed the rulers and authorities [and] made a public display of them, having triumphed over them through Him [Jesus]" (Col. 2:15).

The crucifixion brought the false powers to light. Jesus has ex-posed the powers of darkness (cf. Luke 1:79; 1 Cor. 4:5-6; Col. 1:13). They are, in fact, powerless over the kingdom of Jesus Christ. When the kingdom of God is compared with the kingdom of Satan there is a radical difference. Satan's mask of deception has been torn from him. What looked like triumph for Satan and his followers, the resurrection showed to be folly. The gates of Satan's kingdom are vulnerable and will be battered down by the advancing church of Jesus Christ under the power of God's Holy Spirit working through obedient, dominion-ori-ented Christians (Matt.16:18). Victory for the people of God is certain: not because of their own strength, but because of the strength of the One whom they serve, even Jesus Christ, unto whom all power in heaven and earth has been given, and who is with His people always, even unto the end of the age (28:18–20). The Christian's hope is found in the resurrected Jesus Christ who sits at the right hand of His Father. Present-day Christians are to know the present-day power of that resurrection and act upon it (cf. Phil. 3:10; Rom. 6:5).

If Satan doesn't have as much power as God does, then Satan's human followers also cannot have as much power as God's human followers do, unless the latter voluntarily renounce their responsibilities. If God's people are faithful, power will flow to them (Deut. 28:1–14).

The Question of Time

One of the most debilitating "doctrines" of the church is the belief that Jesus could come back "at any moment," even in our lifetime. History is filled with people making predictions about the last days. A common element binds them together. Each and every one of them has been wrong.[6]

When Jesus' disciples asked Him at the ascension if at that time He was "restoring the kingdom to Israel," Jesus diverted their attention from final restoration to the work at hand: "It is not for you to know times and epochs which the Father has fixed by His own authority; but you shall receive power when the Holy Spirit has come upon you; and you shall be My witnesses both in Jerusalem, and in all Judea and Samaria, and even to the remotest part of the earth" (Acts 1:6–8). In effect, Jesus was saying, "Do not worry about God's timetable; it is already fixed. Busy yourself with the affairs of the kingdom."

Some of the Thessalonian Christians were "leading an undisciplined life, doing no work at all, but acting like busybodies" (2 Thess. 3:11). While this may have little to do with a preoccupation with "the day of the Lord" (1 Thess. 5:2), it reminds us that God requires us to work, regardless of external circumstances. Faithfulness is evaluated in terms of kingdom work: "Who then is the faithful and sensible slave whom his master put in charge of his household to give them their food at the proper time? Blessed is that slave whom his master finds so doing when he comes" (Matt. 24:45–46). Jesus goes on to hint at the time and circumstances of His coming: "the master of that slave will come on a day when he does not expect him and at an hour which he does not know" (24:50).

Nowhere does Scripture intimate that we should cease any aspect of kingdom work, even if we think Jesus' coming is near. George Ladd, a premillennial scholar, writes, "The delay of the master made no difference to the true servant: he busied himself about his Lord's business . . . But the master's delay induced the false servant to a sinful course of action. The Lord's delay brought out the true character of his servants."[7]

Jesus related a parable to His disciples when "they supposed that the kingdom of God was going to appear immediately" (Luke 19:11). In Jesus' day, many of His disciples assumed the kingdom would arrive through a cataclysmic event with no effort on their part. Jesus told them through the parable, "do business until I come back" (19:13). When the master finally returns he will take an accounting. Those who made a profit on the money given by the master will "be in authority over ten and five cities" (19:17–19). The one who put the money "away in a handkerchief" (19:20), not being industrious enough to "put the money in the bank" to collect "interest" (19:23), loses everything (19:24).

Charles Haddon Spurgeon (1834–1892), the great Baptist preacher and evangelist of the nineteenth century, shows how pessimism about the future robs the church of its vitality and stunts its growth.

> David was not a believer in the theory that the world will grow worse and worse, and that the dispensations will wind up with general darkness, and idolatry. Earth's sun is to go down amid tenfold night if some of our prophetic brethren are to be believed. Not so do we expect, but we look for a day when the dwellers in all lands shall learn righteousness, shall trust in the Saviour, shall worship thee alone, God, "and shall glorify thy name." The modern notion has greatly damped the zeal of the church for missions, and the sooner it is shown to be unscriptural the better for the cause of God. It neither consorts with prophecy, honours God, nor inspires the church with ardour. Far hence be it driven."[8]

"Therefore, my beloved brethren, be steadfast, immovable, always abounding in the work of the Lord, knowing that your toil is not in vain in the Lord" (1 Cor. 15:58).

Our Inheritance Grows

Until Christians began to spread the gospel into the Roman Empire, the ancient world had never heard of linear (straight line) time. The ancient pagan world, from savages to sophisticated philosophers, believed in circular time. Time is cyclical, they argued. It is going nowhere. There was no beginning; there will be no end.

Christians challenged this view of time. They preached Christ, and Him crucified. Christ came in the midst of time, they said. God created the world; Adam rebelled; and now Christ has come in the midst of time to die and rise from the dead, overcoming sin. His resurrection points to a future resurrection (1 Cor. 15). Thus, we have hope for the future; only Christians had such hope; therefore, only Christians had enough confidence in the future to preach a doctrine of linear time.

God told His people that their earthly efforts have meaning in time and eternity. What we think, say, and do has consequences for us, and also for history. And we know that the good that we do becomes a legacy to other Christians who follow us. Because we have legitimate faith in the future, we can confidently use other people's gifts to us out of the past. And we know that in the future, our good gifts will be put to good use by our spiritual heirs.

Not so the God-haters. Their gifts will either be cut off, or else be inherited by God's people. "The wealth of the sinner is stored up for the righteous" (Prov. 13:22b). Our God shows lovingkindness to thousands of generations, to those who keep His commandments (Ex. 20:6). The text in Exodus 20 says that He shows lovingkindness to thousands, but most commentators agree that the comparison is between the three or four generations that He patiently endures sinners (20:5) and the thousands of generations of kindness that He shows to the righteous.

We can build up spiritual, economic, educational, and political capital over many generations. This is our task before God. Slow growth over many generations is the proper approach.

Christians who have spoken for the church historically have usually believed in the steady progress of the gospel. They have opposed radical revolution. They have had faith in the future. Nevertheless, in our day too many well-intentioned Christians have dreamed of miracles to change the effects of evil overnight, and others have prayed for the "rapture" to remove them from earthly misery.

It is time to call a halt to this temporary period of Christian pessimism. We must lengthen our time perspectives and then get to work. Consider that, "The Japanese don't ask, 'Will it be viable in five years?' They know it will be viable sometime, so they go ahead and do it. Doesn't anyone in this country realize that 10 years isn't a long time?"[9] We should adopt the perspective of the sixteenth-century reformer John Calvin when it comes to understanding the gospel and the future. As William J. Bouwsma writes:

> "When our Lord Jesus appeared," Calvin declared, "he acquired possession of the whole world; and his kingdom was extended from one end of it to the other, especially with the proclamation of the Gospel. . . . God has consecrated the entire earth through the precious blood of his Son to the end that we may inhabit it *and live under his reign.*" This meant that religious reform pointed also to the reform of the secular realm. "We must not only grieve for the offenses committed by unbelievers," Calvin warned, "but also recognize that we remain unworthy to look upon heaven until there is harmony and unanimity in religion, till God is purely worshipped by all, and *all the world is reformed.*" Believers "truly worship God by the righteousness they maintain within their society."[10]

Ted Peters writes that the effect of pessimism "functions to justify social irresponsibility," and many "find this doctrine a comfort in their lethargy."[11]

Summary Concepts

God tells us that it is our task to subdue the earth to His glory. This will take the cumulative efforts of all His people. No single generation will get all the credit. Step by step, line upon line, here a little and there a little, His kingdom in heaven marches forward, steadily manifesting itself in the kingdoms of this world. We are to pray, "Thy kingdom come. Thy will be done, on earth as it is in heaven." Because we have stopped praying that prayer, or because we no longer believe its words, we have given up too much ground and authority to the satanic enemy.

We have in effect despised the day of small beginnings. We have looked at the task ahead of us and have given up, overwhelmed by its magnitude. We have forgotten that after we do our work and die, there will come generations after us.

The battle for the universe takes place here on earth, not in the grave or in heaven. The battle is spiritual and ethical. It is fought in history. How is it to be fought? Not by power alone, certainly. Not by politics alone. By the preaching of the gospel and obedience to His law.

Summary Principles

1. Christians are far behind the humanists in every area of life.
2. Short of major catastrophes, it will take a long time to regain this lost ground.
3. Christians are not ready to exercise responsibility in the major institutions: education, entertainment, government.
4. Nevertheless, the kingdom of God goes on.
5. Retreat by Christians is a sign of unbelief.
6. Joshua and Caleb alone recommended an offensive against the Canaanites; they alone entered the land 40 years later.
7. The "giants of the land" (humanists) can be defeated.
8. Christians are the main enemies of the humanists today.
9. Politics is too often seen as the fundamental activity for societal change.

10. The State's authority and operations should be drastically reduced.

11. Many Christians don't want to think of the Bible as a guide to government.

12. Non-Christians are equally hostile.

13. The redeemed sinner is to be salt and light to the corrupt culture.

14. Humanism has advanced as Christianity has retreated.

15. Satan doesn't have more power than God.

16. Satan's followers don't have more power than God's followers, unless God's followers give up and give in.

17. God requires us to work, no matter how little time we have remaining.

18. Pessimism concerning the future has robbed the church of its vitality (Spurgeon).

19. The Bible teaches growth over time, generation after generation.

20. The ancient pagan world believed in historical cycles.

21. The Christian should believe in the earthly future, so he should be able to pass on the gifts of the past.

22. The God-haters will be cut off before they see the full development of their culture.

23. Capital in the broadest sense is to be built up over many generations.

24. Satan's followers cannot expect to succeed for many generations, unless Christians hand over the civilization to them.

25. We need revival, not miracles.

26. We need the whole counsel of God.

27. We can get this if we work hard and long, so that God can safely send our culture a spiritual awakening.

28. The Communists believe in overnight revolution, and they work for decades to bring it about.

29. Christians say they believe in the long haul, but give up politically after a short time, trusting instead in an overnight victory in a national election.

Notes

1. D. James Kennedy and Jerry Newcombe, *What if Jesus Had Never Been Born?* (Nashville, TN: Thomas Nelson, 1994 and Alvin J. Schmidt, *Under the Influence: How Christianity Transformed Civilization* (Grand Rapids, MI: Zondervan), 2001).

2. The material from this section is taken from Dennis Prager, "Conservatives have talk radio, liberals have everything else," *WorldNetDaily* (January 7, 2003), www.worldnetdaily.com/news/article.asp?ARTICLE_ID=30360

3. Malcolm Gladwell, *The Tipping Point: How Little Things Can Make a Big Difference* (Boston: Little, Brown and Company, 2000).

4. Gary DeMar, *Last Days Madness: Obsession of the Modern Church*, 4th ed. (Powder Springs, GA: American Vision, 1999) and *End Times Fiction: A Biblical Consideration of the Left Behind Theology* (Nashville, TN: Thomas Nelson, 2000).

5. Gary North, *Unholy Spirits: Occultism and New Age Humanism* (Ft. Worth, Texas: Dominion Press, 1986), 15 and 379.

6. Francis X. Gumerlock, *The Day and the Hour: Christianity's Perennial Fascination with Predicting the End of the World* (Powder Springs, GA: American Vision, 2000).

7. George Eldon Ladd, *The Blessed Hope* (Grand Rapids, Michigan: Eerdmans, 1956), 106.

8. Charles H. Spurgeon, *The Treasury of David*, 7 vols. (Grand Rapids, MI: Guardian Press, [1870–1885] 1976), 4.102.

9. Alan Huang, researcher for AT&T's Bell Laboratories. Quoted in *World* (February 10, 1990), 4.

10. William J. Bouwsma, *John Calvin: A Sixteenth Century Portrait* (New York: Oxford University Press, 1988), 192.

11. Ted Peters, *Futures: Human and Divine* (Atlanta, GA: John Knox, 1978), 28, 29.

Part 2

Is Social Justice Just?

"The smallest good deed is better than the grandest intention."

While "social justice" means different things to different people, generally the term is used to advocate government intervention to bring a nation into economic and social balance. Since there are inequities in the world, advocates of social justice demand that the State, civil government, should be given authority to implement laws and procedures to equalize disparities in income and access to opportunities. The method is to confiscate a large portion of the advantages of the "haves," usually in terms of income, and redistribute these "extra" advantages to the "have-nots." Over time, so the theory goes, differences of income, lifestyle, social status, and educational levels and opportunities will be brought into closer alignment. Economic and social equilibrium will be established. There won't be as many rich or as many poor. Everybody will mostly be in the middle. By calling the process "social *justice*," advocates hope to convey the idea of legitimacy to the process.

In looking for a helpful way to explain the meaning of justice, sports often come to mind. Rarely are teams equal in ability. What if umpires had the jurisdictional authority to rid the playing field of inequities at the request of a manager who believes that the opposing team has better players? Both teams know the rules going into the game. Umpires are present to ensure that the written rules are followed to the letter. As long as the players and coaches follow the rules and umpires enforce the rules, justice prevails even if there are inequities. It is not the job of an umpire (judge) to eliminate disparities. Who would ever want to play the game if the rules are always in flux?

The cry for "social justice" is a call for the State to do something to fix economic and relational inequities without any regard to a universal principle of justice. By describing justice in social rather than *legal* terms, our attention is immediately drawn to national problems that can only be fixed by a civil government with enough power to enforce its policies. So then, advocates of "social justice" believe that the State plays the major role in rectifying so-called social problems because they are national in scope. Antonio Martino points out that the expression: "Social justice . . . owes its immense popularity precisely to its ambiguity and meaninglessness. It can be used by different people, holding quite different views, to designate a wide variety of different things. Its obvious appeal stems from its persuasive strength, from its positive connotations, which allows the user to praise his own ideas and simultaneously express contempt for the ideas of those who don't agree with him."[1]

Anyone who criticizes policies that carry the label "social justice" are immediately considered to be callous, insensitive, uncaring, and lacking in compassion. In reality, however, those who oppose "social justice" policies are not against treating people in a just way. They firmly believe that most if not all social justice policies that involve the State are wrong and, in the long run, do more harm than good.[2] Attaching the "social justice" label to a program does not make it a just and helpful program anymore than attaching a Mercedes Benz hood ornament to a Volkswagen will make it a luxury car.

War on Poverty or War on the Poor?

Foes of sophisticated and expensive governmental programs implemented by distant bureaucratic agencies designed to help the poor may be right on target with their opposition. They have history on their side. Confiscating literally *trillions* of dollars in taxes from one segment of society and redistributing the collected revenue to another segment of society and calling it "social justice" does not mean that it is in fact the *just* thing to do. "Social justice" is not in operation when the State takes upon itself the right to confiscate so-called excess capital from the rich to care for the poor, especially when the Bible opposes confiscatory taxation and such policies do not work. Herbert Schlossberg writes:

> Since government produces no goods, it can distribute only what it takes from others. This process is indistinguishable from theft. When an election, or in some countries a coup, changes the identity of plunderers and plundered, yesterday's injustice becomes today's justice. In a redistributive society, the law is a thief.[3]

Some might object by claiming that since government is doing the confiscating and redistributing, the procedure is legitimate by definition. This is hardly true. At one time slavery was constitutional, women were denied the right to vote, Japanese American citizens were interred during World War II, and legal obstacles were put before blacks making it difficult for them to vote. Because the government did these things did not make them just. Similarly, just because the Supreme Court ruled in 1973 that abortion is constitutional, legal, and a woman's fundamental right does not make the procedure just.

Attempts to solve problems by declaring war on them and throwing money at them by the national government has been an ongoing theme in politics since the mid-1960s. As you might expect, wars are expensive, and there are many casualties. "Overall, civilian social welfare costs increased by twenty times from 1950 to 1980, in constant dollars. During the same period, the United States population increased by half."[4] When the Food Stamp Program began in 1965, 424,000 people participated in the program (that's less than 9,000 people per state, a manageable number for private welfare agencies to handle).[5] At the end of Lyndon Johnson's presidency in 1968, participation increased to 2.2 million. The number doubled during the first two years of Richard Nixon's presidency (1969–70). By the end of Nixon's first term in 1972, the number of food stamp recipients had increased five-fold. "By 1980, more than twenty-one million people were receiving food stamps, fifty times more people than were covered during the Johnson presidency."[6]

Using the State to satisfy a concept of "social justice" did more harm than good because it lured people into programs that made them dependent upon the State. Undoubtedly there were poor people in 1965 who needed food and shelter, but creating a government program in an attempt to satisfy the need was the wrong solution.

Keep in mind that the money actually spent on these programs is only a faction of the money collected.

In 1982, the total U.S. welfare bill at all levels of government (federal, state, and local) came to 403 billion dollars. If we take figures from the Bureau of the Census (August 1984) which state that the number of people living in poverty in the U.S. was 15.2 percent of the population or 35.3 million people, an amazing fact emerges. Had we simply divided the 403 billion dollars this nation spent on poverty at every level of government among the estimated number of poor people, each poor person could have received $11,133. For a family of four, this would have totaled $44,532. Since the official poverty level per family for that year was $9,287, it is clear that America's fight against poverty involves enormous overhead costs. Most of the tax dollars collected to fight poverty end up, Thomas Sowell notes, "in the pockets of highly paid administrators, consultants, and staff as well as higher-income recipients of benefits from programs advertised as anti-poverty efforts." Clearly, the bucket used to carry money from the pockets of the taxpayer to the poor is leaking badly. Many think the real beneficiaries of liberal social programs are not the poor and disadvantaged but the members of the governmental bureaucracy who administer the program.[7]

Those who administer these programs have a vested interest in their survival and expansion. Winning the war on poverty is not the goal, perpetuating the programs is. "Less than 25 percent of all the tax dollars allocated to fight poverty at every level of government reaches the poor. The other 75 percent goes to pay overhead."[8]

Advocates of "social justice" programs implemented by the State at the expense of the mainly productive members of society will claim that there are success stories. Few would dispute the claim. When so much money is being poured into these programs, someone is bound to benefit. But if that same money—including the revenue lost in overhead expenditures that never reach the poor—were saved, invested, and spent instead of taxed, many more people would benefit, and we would have fewer social-welfare slaves.

Biblical Justice

The State's job is to establish justice in terms of *biblical* law; its job is not to equalize the disparities between rich and poor, the goal of many advocates of "social justice." If a businessman is cheating a customer by lying about his product and tampering with its weight or fineness, the State has jurisdiction to act: "You shall have just balances, just weights, a just epha [bushel], and a just hin [gallon]: I am the Lord your God, who brought you out of the land of Egypt" (Lev. 19:36); "A just balance and scales belong to the LORD; all the weights of the bag are His concern" (Prov. 16:11). This is called *commercial justice.*

The State also has jurisdiction over criminal acts, what is called *remedial justice.* The Bible is filled with examples of how the State should function in this regard (e.g., Ex. 23:3–6). To give the State jurisdiction to operate in the nebulous realm of *social justice* is to give the State more power than God has ordained it to have. In essence, the State becomes a god because there are no fixed laws that one can turn to in order to set boundaries for the State's actions to determine what's an inequity. "Because human nature is corrupt, the traditionalist resists the concentration of power in any single institution or person. No one institution should be regarded as sovereign outside of its own legitimate, but strictly limited, sphere. Society in this perspective is a matrix of competing sovereignties, each with certain claims on men, but none with total claims in all areas."[9] If a decentralized social order with competing, legitimate, God-ordained sovereignties is not maintained, tyranny is the result.

The State as Messiah

William F. Buckley captures the essence of the people's preoccupation with the divinized state: "If there is crime in the street, it is because government does not provide enough day care. If there is unemployment in the steel mills, it is because the government is using too much steel making submarines. If there is a growing number of broken homes, it is because government has not passed the Equal Rights Amendment. If there is tension owing to Soviet deployment of missiles in Europe, it is because the government has failed to lie down with Moscow, as with a lamb."[10] We can continue the litany: If there is child abuse, it is because government does not make abortion an easier alternative. If teenagers are having babies outside of marriage, it is because the government has not made more free contraceptives available. If tests scores are declining, it is because the government does not give enough money to education.

Politicians pick up on the theme of dependency and use it for great political gain: "The idol state uses the language of compassion because its intention is a messianic one. It finds the masses harassed and helpless, like sheep without a shepherd, needing a savior."[11]

Conclusion

An additional point needs to be made. While good intentions should be commended, good intentions have little to do with what is actually just and helpful for those truly in need. There is no question that most advocates of a "social justice" perspective care about the poor. "But their compassion is often wedded to a political and economic ideology that is long on heart and short on wisdom. The emotional side of

Christian social concern—loving and caring—is only half the story. The best of intentions cannot actually aid the poor unless channeled into actions that are informed by sound economic theory and practice. When 'aid' is grounded on bad economics, it will usually make any bad situation worse."[12]

Notes

1. Antonio Martino, "The Myth of Social Justice," in *Three Myths* by Arnold Beichman, Antonio Martino, and Kenneth Minogue (Washington, D.C.: The Heritage Foundation, 1982), 23. Quoted in Ronald H. Nash, *Social Justice and the Christian Church* (Milford, Michigan: Mott Media, 1983), 5–6.

2. "AFDC was to take care of widows with small children. . . . Nothing in the New Deal [Social Security, Aid to Families with Dependent Children (AFDC), Workman's Compensation, and Unemployment Insurance] provided help just because a person was poor or hampered by social disadvantages. . . . By the fifties it had become embarrassingly, outrageously clear that most of [the women receiving benefits] were not widows. Many of them had not even been married. Worst of all, they didn't stop having babies after the first lapse. They kept having more. This had not been part of the plan." (Charles Murray, *Losing Ground: American Social Policy, 1950–1980* [New York: Basic Books, 1984], 17–18).

3. Herbert Schlossberg, *Idols for Destruction: The Conflict of Christian Faith and American Culture* (Wheaton, IL: Crossway Books, [1983] 1993), 118.

4. Murray, *Losing Ground*, 14.

5. Typically social welfare programs begin small, but before too long, they expand well beyond their initial intended purpose. When a behavior is subsidized, you get more of it.

6. Ronald H. Nash, *Poverty and Wealth: The Christian Debate Over Capitalism* (Westchester, Illinois: Crossway Books, 1986), 176.

7. Nash, *Poverty and Wealth*, 177.

8. Ronald H. Nash, *Why the Left is Not Right: The Religious Left—Who They Are and What They Believe* (Grand Rapids, Michigan: Zondervan, 1996), 183.

9. Gary North, *An Introduction to Christian Economics* (Nutley, New Jersey: The Craig Press, 1973), 226.

10. "For the Democrats, Government is a God," *The Atlanta Journal* (July 23, 1984), 9A.

11. Schlossberg, *Idols for Destruction*, 185.

12. Nash, *Social Justice and the Christian Church*, 3.

Making Terrorist Connections

"Off the Pigs!"
"Personally I always held my flower in a clenched fist."
"Yippies[1] believe in the violation of every law."

—Abbie Hoffman (1936–1989)

Soon after Timothy McVeigh bombed the Alfred P. Murrah federal building in Oklahoma City in April of 1995, some on the left of the political spectrum blamed "anti-government rhetoric" for the assault. Supposedly "hateful" speech directed at politicians had incited a cadre of "right-wing" extremists to put words into explosive action. Is any of this true? Did angry white males give up on the democratic process, abandon moral precepts, and resort to revolutionary rhetoric and incendiary devices to vent their anger against an ever increasing power-hungry government? The facts do not support the shaky premises. For one thing, the conservative agenda has always been to bring about social, cultural, and political change through the democratic process, not through revolution.

A similar blame-game tactic was tried by South Dakota Democrat Senator Tom Daschle after the loss of the Senate to the Republicans in the 2002 mid-term elections. He blamed their losses on "talk radio" listeners who "want to act" in ways that would threaten those in "public life." Editorial writers compared American "fundamentalist" Christians to Islamic extremists.[2] Like so many, Daschle and other critics offered no empirical evidence to back up their claims. As Dick Williams observed, "if U.S. senators and their families have been threatened with violence, the press and the police have kept it a secret."[3]

Liberals cannot claim that "talk radio" hosts were responsible for getting angry Americans to the voting booth (a good thing) and at the same time blame radio rhetoric for inciting a few disturbed individuals to bomb a government building (a bad thing). The two actions are mutually exclusive. There is no evidence that McVeigh's revolutionary act was inspired by what he heard on talk radio.

Power Grows Out of the Barrel of a Gun

Using violence to bring about societal and cultural change has been a standard tool of the political left. Mao Tse Tung's revolutionary manifesto that "power grows out of a barrel of a gun" is a slogan adopted by leftist revolutionaries. Leaders of student movements in the 1960s used the rhetoric of violence and acted on it to further their anti-establishment cause. Carl Oglesby, president of the ultra-leftist Students for a Democratic Society (SDS), said, "Revolutions do not take place in velvet boxes. . . . Nuns will be raped and bureaucrats will be disemboweled."[4] Some of his revolutionary followers took him seriously.

Déjà Vu All Over Again

In the 1960s, Columbia University and other major universities were marked by student sit-ins. The catalyst for student rebellion that swept the nation in the tumultuous decade was the Berkeley "Free Speech Movement" (FSM). The FSM was decidedly anti-establishment, painting university personnel as "repressive autocrats lurking behind a benign mask of liberalism."[5] Authority was questioned at every opportunity. The police were described as "pigs," accomplices of the establishment rather than enforcers of the law that was supposed to apply to everyone without distinction.

The counter culture decade of the 1960s was described as the "decade of anger and rebellion." While most channeled their anger in constructive ways, some went off the deep end and turned to violent measures. Sit-ins led to explosions when anti-war activists planted a fertilizer and fuel oil bomb at Sterling Hall, home of the University of Wisconsin's Physics Department and the Army Math Research Center. The explosion killed a graduate student. Violence begat violence when four students were killed by National Guardsmen on the campus of Kent State University on May 4, 1970. Student protesters had set fire to an ROTC building and thrown bottles at police.

Bloody Labor

People associated with fringe political groups, mostly on the left side of the political spectrum, have often taken the revolutionary road of violence. For example, the history of the labor movement in this country is one of purposeful disorder outside the bounds of the political process. "As it entered the industrial age full blast in the 1870s, America had plunged into 'the bloodiest and most violent labor history of any industrial nation in the world.'"[6] Under the auspices of the first Education and Defense Society, "workers met regularly and drilled with firearms."[7] On May 4, 1886, during a labor rally in Chicago's Haymarket Square, anarchists had thrown a bomb into police ranks, killing 7 policemen and injuring 70 more. The gathering had been organized to protest the killing of six striking workers at the McCormick harvester plant.

At the trial for the anarchist leaders, the following treatise, written by Johann Most, a leading American anarchist, was entered into evidence: *Science of Revolutionary War Manual for Instruction in the Use and Preparation of Nitro-Glycerine, Dynamite, Gun-Cotton, Fulminating Mercury, Bombs, Fuses, Poisons, and so forth.*[8] Most's guide consisted of information he gathered from his experience at an explosives' factory in

Jersey City. "With a certain zest he contemplated using 'hand grenades and blasting cartridges ... the proletariat's substitute for artillery.' Larger bombs were even more promising: 'That which reduces what had been solid rocks into splinters may not have a bad effect in a court or a monopolist's ballroom.'"[9] Like all romantic revolutionaries, Most believed that humanity could be saved only "with blood and iron, poison and dynamite!"[10] As one would expect, "the Haymarket incident hurt the labor movement by associating it in public opinion with violence and revolution."[11]

In 1912, because of a dispute over unionization, the *Los Angeles Times* building was dynamited and 21 persons killed. "Sixteen packets of bombs were found in the New York Post Office in April 1919. In June 1919, bombs damaged the houses of the U.S. attorney general, the mayor of Cleveland and judges in New York and Boston."[12] In September 1920, a group of anti-capitalist anarchists set off a bomb on Wall Street, killing 38 people.

Building a Guerrilla Force

By the late 1960s and early 1970s, there was a resurgence of left-wing radicalism that led to violence. On May 7, 1967, just weeks before the Newark riot, Greg Calvert, a member of Students for a Democratic Society, described its members as "post-communist revolutionaries" who "are working to build a guerrilla force in an urban environment. We are actively organizing sedition."[13] The SDS was a growing radical movement made up of college students. The rhetoric of the SDS was at its core anti-government and anti-establishment. "SDS organizers denounced 'oppressors,' 'exploiters,' and 'the Al Capones who run this country.' The university was depicted as a 'colony' of 'the military-industrial complex' and a 'midwife to murder.' 'Imperialism' was offered as a convenient scapegoat for every frustration and failure."[14] A keynote speech at a 1962 SDS convention praised the freedom riders, not for furthering civil rights but for their "radicalizing" potential, their "clear-cut demonstration for the sterility of legalism." The speaker continued:

It is not by . . . "learning the rules of the legislative game" that we will succeed in creating the kind of militant alliances that our struggle requires. We shall succeed through force—through the exertion of such pressure as will force our reluctant allies to accommodate to us, in their own interest.[15]

Tom Hayden, a former SDS organizer and strategist, member of the California General Assembly, and one-time husband of Jane Fonda, intoned the following in 1967: "Perhaps the only forms of action appropriate to the angry people are violent. Perhaps a small minority, by setting ablaze New York and Washington, could damage this country forever in the court of world opinion. Urban guerrillas are the only realistic alternative at this time to electoral politics or mass armed resistance."[16] Hayden's tactics predated those of the Islamic estremists who flew two fuel-laden jet liners into the World Trade Towers on September 11, 2001.

"Burn, Baby, Burn"

Tom Hayden's anti-government, revolutionary rhetoric bordered on the fringes of sedition and treason. His speech inflamed so many radical extremists that some blame him for agitating fragile race relations in Newark, New Jersey, causing nearly a week of rioting in the summer of 1967. While Hayden was not directly involved, he seemed to approve of using violence as a way of "shattering the status quo." The August 24, 1967, issue of *The New York Review of Books* includes an article in which Hayden wrote:

The role of organized violence is now being carefully considered. During a riot, for instance, a conscious guerrilla can participate in pulling police away from the path of people engaged in attacking stores. He can create disorder in new areas the police think are secure. He can carry the torch, if not all the people, to white neighborhoods and downtown business districts. If necessary, he can successfully shoot to kill.

The guerrilla can employ violence effectively during times of apparent "peace," too. He can attack, in the suburbs or slums, with paint or bullets, symbols of racial oppression.

These tactics of disorder will be defined by the authorities as criminal anarchy. But it may be that disruption will create possibilities of meaningful change. . . . Violence can contribute to shattering the status quo, but only politics and organization can transform it.[17]

Nearly two thousand people were arrested during the Newark strife. Snipers killed a policeman, and police responded with wild gunfire, killing a 74-year-old bystander and wounding others. When the anarchy subsided, twenty-four people had been killed. The chaos did not stop with sniper fire and looting. The Newark Fire Department recorded 122 fires in the first twenty-four hours of the riots. A total of 250 fires were set, thirteen of which were considered serious.

In 1967 Detroit became a war zone. In five days firebugs ignited an estimated 225 buildings. Wind-whipped flames burned twice that many more. The rhetorical goal of these revolutionaries was supposedly a reaction to past injustices and a desire to build a better society on the remaining ashes. But actions speak louder than words. "The cities burned, while the kids kicked in the windows, cut hoses, and danced in the streets. The nation watched them on the evening news, black faces shining in the glare of fires, grinning as they passed TV's and cases of liquor out through the broken windows—scattering down dark streets— falling occasionally to a guardsman's shot. And their elders, whites, and many blacks as well, shuddered at the nihilistic new litany that welled up now in place of 'We Shall Overcome': *Burn, Baby, Burn!*"[18]

"Che Lives!"

A student from the University of California at Berkeley stated that she understood why certain groups riot. "I feel the same frustrations in myself, the same urge to violence."[19] The campus at Berkeley led the way. In 1967 the national secretary of SDS declared himself to be a disciple of Che Guevera: "Che's message is applicable to urban America as far as the psychology of guerrilla action goes. . . . Che sure lives in our hearts." He added that "Black power is absolutely necessary." White student activists noted that "black nationalists are stacking Molotov cocktails and studying how they can hold a few city blocks in an uprising, how to keep off the fire brigade and the police so that the National Guard must be called out. . . ."[20]

In the July 11, 1968, issue of *The Village Voice*, Marvin Garson, the pamphleteer of the Free Speech Movement, recounted with pride the bombings which had been the calling card of campus radicals from Berkeley and its environs:

> The series of successful and highly popular bombings which have occurred here recently: the steady bombing of the electric power system from mid-March when the lines leading to the Lawrence Radiation Lab were knocked down, to June 4, when on the morning of the California primary 300,000 homes in Oakland were cut off; the dynamiting of a bulldozer engaged in urban renewal destruction of Berkeley's funkiest block; three separate bombings of the Berkeley draft board; and finally, last Tuesday night, the dynamiting of the checkpoint kiosk at the western entrance to the University campus, a symbol of the Board of Regent's property rights in the community of scholars.[21]

Civil unrest and purposeful destruction of the nation's infrastructure and authority institutions was the order of the day in the late 1960s. "On September 3, 1968, *The New York Times* reported that the city of Berkeley was declared to be in a state of civil disaster; the city authorities invoked emergency police powers, and the campus of the university was placed under curfew rules.[22]

The left-wing radical Weathermen were even more militant. They too were into bombs. Fortunately, they were also inept. "On March 6,

1970, a tremendous explosion demolished a fashionable Greenwich Village townhouse, and from the flaming wreckage fled two SDS 'Weatherwomen,' members of the SDS terrorist faction. In the rubble police found remains of a 'bomb factory' and three bodies, including one of the organizers of the 1968 Columbia University rioting and another of a 'regional traveler' who had helped spark the Kent State buildup. Four days later in Maryland two close associates of Student Non-Violent Coordinating Committee (SNCC) firebrand 'Rap' Brown blew themselves to smithereens while apparently transporting a bomb to the courthouse where their cohort was to stand trial on an inciting riot charge. . . . Also, in 1970 a Black Panther carrying a bomb along a Minneapolis street blasted himself to bits. Despite the carnage to themselves, Panther and Weatherman terrorists succeeded in setting off bombs in the New York City police headquarters, the U.S. Capitol, and scores of other public and corporate buildings across the nation."[23] In addition, they had succeeded in setting off bombs in the Pentagon and several major courthouses. "These were the bombings they took credit for publicly. The full extent of their terrorist activities remains unknown."[24]

Did you notice the targets?: New York City police headquarters, the U.S. Capitol, and the Pentagon. Do the attacks on these American symbols remind you of anything? Islamic terrorists are followed a similar but more destructive long-term goal. First it was the Communists. Capitalistic and Christian America stood in the way of Communism's utopian dream of a classless society. The shoe-pounding Nikita Kruschev was upfront about what he had in store for America: "We will bury you." Then it was the leftist campus radicals who convinced themselves that the "establishment," the military industrial complex, and the "system" stood in the way of their illusionary Woodstock dream of perpetual peace and love.

Now we have a more insidious and resolute enemy. The publication of an al-Qaeda manifesto, translated by the Middle East Research Institute (MEMRI), makes its agenda clear and concise: A Muslim 'knows that his nation was created to stand at the center of leadership, at the center of hegemony and rule, at the center of ability and sacrifice.

. . . [H]e knows that the [divine] rule is that the entire earth must be subject to the religion of Allah—not to the East, not to the West—to no ideology and to no path except the path of Allah." The goal of the radical Islamists is the universal triumph of Islam and the obliteration of all obstacles that stand in the way of achieving that end. David Horowitz's comments are on the mark:

> This is not a war about land in the Middle East or the structure of a Palestinian state, or a U.S. military presence in the Arabian peninsula. It is a war about redemption. In this it exactly parallels the Communist threat from the past. In the eyes of the Communists, America stood in the way of heaven—a socialist paradise in which racism, sexism, and economic inequality would vanish from the earth. In the eyes of radical Islam, America—the Great Satan—stands in the way of Islam's rule, and thus of human redemption and it is for this reason America must be destroyed.
>
> Thus, the al-Qaeda proclamation: "America is the head of heresy in our modern world, and it leads an infidel democratic regime that is based upon separation of religion and state and on ruling the people by the people via legislating laws that contradict the way of Allah and permit what Allah has prohibited. This compels the other countries to act in accordance with the same laws in the same ways . . . and punishes any country [that rebels against these laws] by besieging it, and then by boycotting it. By so doing [America] seeks to impose on the world a religion that is not Allah's."[25]

America, according to Islamic extremists, is an infidel nation, officially atheistic and murderous.

While Christians recognize that America is apostate and many of its laws unjust and immoral, they do not call for violent revolution to bring about social, cultural, and political change. With the reformation of the individual comes the reformation of society. Unfortunately, many

Christians have given up on any hope of moral and cultural restoration. In their way of seeing things, the world is predetermined to be evil and destined toward apocalypticism. The Islamists are perceived as one of God's end-time prophetic players to prepare the world for the "rapture." While the Islamists are preparing to create a world without Christians, Christians are hoping that an end-time event will remove them before all hell breaks loose.[26]

Revolution for the Hell of It

On the cover of *Revolution for the Hell of It*, Abbie Hoffman,[27] the late Yippie spokesman of the 1960s, is pictured with a rifle in his hand leaping for joy. Since Hoffman was something of a jokester, some might claim that an armed and jubilant Hoffman gracing the cover of a book was nothing more than a satirical barb at the establishment. The content of the book tells a different story. Hoffman envisioned and encouraged today's sexual revolution and the general disembowelment of morality. Hoffman went further by supplying information that he hoped would lead to the violent overthrow of "the system":

> To enter the twenty-first century, to have revolution in our lifetime, male supremacy must be smashed, . . . A militant Gay Liberation Front has taught us that our stereotypes of masculinity were molded by the same enemies of life that drove us out of Lincoln Park. The words "chick" and "fag" and the deep-rooted attitudes they imply must be purged from the New Nation. Cultural Revolution means a disavowal of the values; all values held by our parents who inhabit and sustain the decaying institutions of a dying Pig Empire.[28]

Hoffman's rhetoric about revolution was just a warm-up. In *Steal This Book* he gave instructions on how to build stink bombs, smoke bombs, sterno bombs, aerosol bombs, pipe bombs, and Molotov Cocktails. Hoffman's updated version of the Molotov Cocktail consisted of a glass bottle filled with a mixture of gasoline and styrofoam, turning the slushy blend into a poor man's version of napalm. The flaming gasoline-soaked styrofoam was designed to stick to policemen when it exploded.[29] Helpful drawings on how to make the incendiary devices are included.

Let's Blow Up Something!

In *Woodstock Nation*, Hoffman updated his revolutionary tactics. This time, Random House is the publisher. Next to Random House's name on the title page, there is an illustration of a man using dynamite to blow up a house. This same illustration first appeared in Hoffman's *Steal This Book*, which was first published by Pirate Editions. "The logo for Pirate Editions displayed the Random House cottage in the process of being demolished by a bomb, and in the foreground a revolutionary who looked a lot like Abbie setting off the explosion."[30] The theme of both books is how to blow up the system, literally. Hoffman informs us that "the best material available on military tactics in revolutionary warfare" is available through "the U.S. Government Printing Office, Washington, D.C."

Another publication that's probably the most valuable work of its kind available is called *Physical Security* and has more relevant information than Che Guevara's *Guerilla Warfare*. The chapter on Sabotage is extremely precise and accurate with detailed instructions on the making of all sorts of homemade bombs and triggering mechanisms. That information, combined with *Army Installations in the Continental United States* and a lot of guts, can really get something going.[31]

Of course, Hoffman never advocates blowing up anything or anyone. "I ain't saying you should use any of this information, in fact for the records of the FBI, I say right now 'Don't blow up your local draft board or other such holy places.' You wouldn't want to get the Government Printing Office indicted for conspiracy, would you now?"[32] He's just making the information available. You know, freedom of expression and all of that. Then he reproduces pages from the *Department of the Army Field Manual* dealing with "Disguised Incendiary Devices," "Mechanical Delay Devices," and pipe bombs.[33]

Short and Selective Memories

Liberals have short and selective memories. "Righteous violence" was rationalized by the front-line New Left leadership in the 1960s in the same way that it is rationalized by those who want us to "understand the plight of Islamic extremists."

The use of violence was justified, many in the New Left comforted themselves, because theirs was a violence to end all violence, a liberating and righteous violence that would rid the world of a system that deformed and destroyed people. Such glorious ends justified, even ennobled, violent means.[34]

Organizations like Students for a Democratic Society (SDS) and the Student Nonviolent Coordinating Committee (SNCC) used violent rhetoric almost from their inception in the early 1960s. John Lewis, the very liberal Democrat representative from Georgia, boasted when he addressed the March on Washington in August 1963, "We will march through the South, . . . the way Sherman did. We shall pursue our own 'scorched earth' policy and burn Jim Crow to the ground—nonviolently. We shall crack the South into a thousand pieces and put them back together in the image of democracy."[35]

Helter Skelter

If this isn't enough, there is a bizarre link between the Weathermen, the SDS, and Charles Manson. Bernardine Dohrn, a Weatherman who made the FBI's Ten Most Wanted list, told an SDS convention just before she went underground: "Offing those rich pigs with their own forks and knives, and then eating a meal in the same room, far out! The Weathermen dig Charles Manson."[36] For a time Manson was the darling of anti-war protester Jerry Rubin. Rubin wrote of Manson in *We Are Everywhere*: "His words and courage inspired us. . . . Manson's soul is easy to touch because it lays quite bare on the surface."[37] Rubin later admitted that he was angered by Manson's "incredible male chauvinism." High praises for ritualistic, political murder but indignation for male chauvinism. Typical. A reporter for the Los Angeles *Free Press* expressed similar sentiments when he found out that Manson was "both anti-Jewish and anti-black."[38]

Why did some on the radical left see Manson as a hero? Perhaps because Manson articulated the same rhetoric of violence that spewed forth from the SDS and Weathermen and actually put it into action as way to bring down "the system." Manson believed that the Tate-LaBianca murders he orchestrated would start a race war.

That Manson foresaw a war between the blacks and the whites was not fantastic. Many people believe that such a war may someday occur. What *was* fantastic was that he was convinced he could personally start that war himself—that by making it look as if blacks had murdered the seven Caucasian victims he could turn the white community against the black community.[39]

Manson had simply acted upon the radical revolutionary tactics that Tom Hayden, Huey Newton, and Bernardine Dohrn had been suggesting for quite some time.

Conclusion

It is significant that Timothy McVeigh and Islamic extremists shared the rhetoric of 1960s radicals and their predecessors. Two years before he blew up the Morrow building, McVeigh wrote a letter to the *Union-Sun & Journal* (Lockport, New York): "We have no proverbial tea to dump; should we instead sink a ship full of Japanese imports? Is a civil war imminent? Do we have to shed blood to reform the current system? I hope it doesn't come to that, but it might." Compare McVeigh's rhetoric with that of Hayden: "Violence can contribute to shattering the status quo."

The bombing of the federal building in Oklahoma City was a desperate and radical response directed at "the establishment." It's conformity to liberal resistance tactics is frightening, but no liberal reporter is likely to make the connection. The ideological and political Left has worked too long to establish itself as a social and cultural force to admit that its history is filled with incendiary rhetoric and real violence.

There are equally revolutionary and violent groups at large in America. We mustn't forget radical environmental organizations like Earth First!, the Animal Liberation Front (ALF), and the Earth Liberation Front (ELF). ELF "uses direct action in the form of economic sabotage to stop the exploitation and destruction of the natural environment." The clandestine members of ELF burn down "luxury houses," torch SUVs at automobile dealerships, set fire to ski resorts, and trash golf courses, all in the name of "saving the planet." Where does the intent to save the planet by violent means stop?

Notes

1. Yippie: "Youth International Party," an anti-establishment worldview. The acronym came before the name and was a corruption of the over used and media-created "hippie." See Terry H. Anderson, *The Movement and the Sixties: Protest in America from Greensboro to Wounded Knee* (New York: Oxford University Press, 1995), 217.

2. Daschle was not alone in his guilt by association tactic: Barbara Ehrenreich, "Christian Wahhabists," *Progressive* (January 2002); Thomas Friedman, "The real war is against religious totalitarianism," *Atlanta Journal and Constitution* (November 27, 2001), A15; and Anthony Lewis, "Hail and Farewell," *New York Times* (December 15, 2001). For responses, see Gene Edward Veith, "Christians as Taliban," *World* (January 19, 2002), 14 and Gary DeMar, "Nzis on Parade," *Biblical Worldview* (March 2002).

3. Dick Williams, "Daschle's attack on talk radio is silly, out of touch with reality," *Atlanta Business Chronicle* (November 22, 2002).

4. In a speech by Carl Oglesby at the Washington Peace March, November 27, 1965. Quoted in Os Guinness, *The Dust of Death: The Sixties Counterculture and How It Changed America Forever* (Wheaton, IL: Crossway Books, 1994), 112.

5. Stanley Rothman and S. Robert Lichter, *Roots of Radicalism: Jews, Christians, and the New Left* (New York: Oxford University Press, 1982), 18.

6. James H. Billington, *Fire in the Minds of Men: Origins of the Revolutionary Faith* (New York: Basic Books, 1980), 433.

7. Billington, *Fire in the Minds of Men*, 433.

8. Billington, *Fire in the Minds of Men*, 437.

9. Billington, *Fire in the Minds of Men*, 437.

10. Quoted in Billington, *Fire in the Minds of Men*, 437.

11. "Haymarket Riot," *NSA Family Encyclopedia*, a special edition of *New Standard Encyclopedia* (Chicago, IL: Standard Educational Corp., 1991), 7:95.

12. Michael Barone, "A Brief history of zealotry in America," *U.S. News & World Report* (May 8, 1995), 45.

13. *New York Times* (May 7, 1967). Quoted in Eugene H. Methvin, *The Rise of Radicalism: The Social Psychology of Messianic Extremism* (New Rochelle, NY: Arlington House, 1973), 497 and *The Riot Makers: The Technology of Social Demolition* (New Rochelle, New York: Arlington House, 1970), 27.

14. Methvin, *Rise of Radicalism*, 504.

15. Thomas Kahn, "The Political Significance of the Freedom Riders," in Mitchell Cohen and Dennis Hale, eds., *The New Student Left* (Boston, Massachusetts: Beacon Press, 1966), 59, 63. Quoted in Rothman and Lichter, *Roots of Radicalism*, 13.

16. Quoted in Methvin, *Rise of Radicalism*, 505.

17. Quoted in *Riot Makers*, 51.

18. Anthony Esler, *Bombs, Beards, and Barricades: 150 years of Youth in Revolt* (New York: Stein and Day, 1971), 271.

19. Lewis S. Feuer, *The Conflict of Generations: The Character and Significance of Student Movements* (New York: Basic Books, 1969), 478.

20. Feuer, *The Conflict of Generations*, 478.

21. Quoted in Feuer, *The Conflict of Generations*, 479.

22. Feuer, *The Conflict of Generations*, 479.

23. Methvin, *Rise of Radicalism*, 513.

24. Rothman and Lichter, *Roots of Radicalism*, 42.

25. David Horowitz, "Know the Enemy (And What He Believes), *Frongpage Magazine Online* (June 24, 2002).

26. Gary DeMar, *Last Days Madness: Obsession of the Modern Church*, 4th ed. (Powder Springs, GA: American Vision, 1999) and *End Times Fiction: A Biblical Consideration of the Left Behind Theology* (Nashville, TN: Thomas Nelson, 2001).

27. Hoffman was found dead in his apartment in April 1989. ("A Flower in a Clenched Fist," *Time* [April 24, 1989], 23).

28. Free (Abbie Hoffman), *Revolution for the Hell of It* (New York: Pocket Books, [1968] 1970), 3.

29. Abbie Hoffman, *Steal This Book* (New York: Pirate Editions, 1971), 170–79.

30. Jack Hoffman and Daniel Simon, *Run, Run, Run: The Lives of Abbie Hoffman* (New York: Jeremy P. Tarcher/Putnam, 1994), 165.

31. Abbie Hoffman, *Woodstock Nation: A Talk-Rock Album* (New York: Random House, 1969), 114.

32. Hoffman, *Woodstock Nation*, 114.

33. Hoffman, *Woodstock Nation*, 115–116.

34. Richard J. Ellis, *The Dark Side of the Left: Illiberal Egalitarianism in America* (Lawrence, KS: University Press of Kansas, 1997), 137.

35. John Lewis, "A Serious Revolution," in Massimo Teodori, ed., *The New Left: A Documentary History* (Indianapolis, IN: Bobbs-Merrill, 1969), 102.

36. Vincent Bugliosi, with Curt Gentry, *Helter Skelter: The True Story of the Manson Murders* (New York: W.W. Norton & Company, 1974), 222. Rothman and Lichter tell it a little differently in *Roots of Radicalism*: "Dig it: First they killed those pigs, then they ate dinner in the same room with them, then they even shoved a fork into the victim's stomach. Wild!" (42).

37. Jerry Rubin, *We Are Everywhere* (New York: Harper & Row, 1971). Quoted in Bugliosi and Gentry, *Helter Skelter*, 221–22.

38. Bugliosi and Gentry, *Helter Skelter*, 222.

39. Bugliosi and Gentry, *Helter Skelter*, 222.

The End of Law

"Unless the Lord builds the house, they labor in vain who build it";
unless the LORD guards the city, the watchman keeps awake in vain"
(Psalm 127:1).

On June 28, 1787, Benjamin Franklin delivered a stirring speech to those in attendance at the Constitutional Convention in Philadelphia. His words then are no less true today. In fact, they struck a profound prophetic note that serve as a disturbing warning to all who would dismiss God's "Sovereignty Over the Nations":

> All of us who were engaged in the struggle [in the war for independence] must have observed frequent instances of a superintending Providence in our favor. To that kind Providence we owe this happy opportunity of consulting in peace on the means of establishing our future national felicity. And have we now forgotten that powerful Friend? Or do we imagine we no longer need His assistance? I have lived . . . a long time, and the longer I live, the more convincing proofs I see of this truth--that God Governs in the affairs of men. And if a sparrow cannot fall to the ground without His notice,[1] is it probable that an empire

can rise without His aid? We have been assured, sir, in the Sacred Writings, that 'except the Lord build the house, they labor in vain that build it.'[2] I firmly believe this; and I also believe that without His concurring aid we shall succeed in this political building no better than the builders of Babel.

Franklin was not known as orthodox in his religious beliefs, but there is no doubt that he understood what made nations great. It wasn't geography, natural resources, or monetary prosperity. The self-taught candlemaker's son, author of *Poor Richard's Almanac*, inventor of the lightning rod and bifocals, and world traveler knew that the key to national success was the acknowledgment that God establishes empires, and He requires that they be built in a certain way. In practical terms alone, Franklin reasoned that to exclude God in nation building is to discount long-term national success.

George Washington offered similar counsel in his Thanksgiving Proclamation of October 3, 1789, just after approving the language of the First Amendment. The Proclamation stated in unequivocal terms that "It is the duty of all nations to acknowledge the providence of Almighty God, to obey His will, to be grateful for His benefits, and humbly to implore His protection and favor." Later in the body of the document, Washington describes God as the "great Lord and Ruler of Nations."[3] Franklin, Washington, and even Jefferson understood that without a sovereign lawgiver there is no basis for good government, legitimate justification for an agreed upon moral order and "those rights which God and the laws have given equally and independently to all."[4] There is nothing in their writings that suggests that there might be other options as some of their contemporaries a continent away proposed.

The thinkers of the Enlightenment planned the rebuilding of society on rational lines. Religion and tradition were seen to have no authority to dictate what the future world should be like. Where they conflicted with human interests they should give way.[5]

Certainly there was no unanimous consensus on religious sentiments, but there was almost unanimous agreement that morality was rooted in religion, even among those like Jefferson who had their squabbles with the church. The Constitution is not a document of law. It says nothing about what constitutes murder or theft. The Constitution implements whatever moral or amoral worldview in vogue. At the time of its drafting, Christianity was considered to be the foundation of a sound moral and political order even though debates raged over particular doctrinal beliefs. In his dissenting opinion in *McGowan v. Maryland*, William O. Douglas stated:

> The institutions of our society are founded on the belief that there is an authority higher than the authority of the State; that there is a moral law which the State is powerless to alter; that the individual possesses rights, conferred by the Creator, which government must respect. The Declaration of Independence stated the now familiar theme: "We hold these Truths to be self-evident, that all Men are created equal, that they are endowed by their Creator with certain unalienable Rights, that among these are Life, Liberty, and the Pursuit of Happiness." And the body of the Constitution as well as the Bill of Rights enshrined those principles.[6]

In Article VII, the constitutional framers acknowledged that their work was "Done in Convention of the Unanimous Consent of the States present the Seventeenth Day of September in the Year of our Lord one thousand seven hundred and Eighty seven and of the Independence of the United States of America the Twelfth."[7] There was no attempt to distance the newly formed nation from its Christian history. To repeat, this did not mean that there was agreement on doctrinal issues or the proper balanced relationship between religion and politics.

The inclusion of "in the Year of our Lord" might seem trivial, conventional, and inconsequential to us, but when compared to what the French did, its implications are immediately understood. The French removed every vestige of religion from their government. A new calendar, developed by Joseph-Louis Lagrange and adopted in 1793 by the new government in France, abolished the seven-day creation week and replaced it with a ten-day scientific (metric) week. Reason, absent of any acknowledgment of revelation, was declared to be god. Robespierre proposed a new civil religion and organized the Festival of the Supreme Being, "whose true priest . . . is nature." The calendar was revised so that it started with a new year one. (The same thing was done in the movie *Rosemary's Baby* at the birth of the antichrist Adrian.) Christ was no longer the center of history. The ethical implications of the French Revolution's rationalistic faith were immediate. The state determined what was reasonable, and it was reasonable (and god-like) to execute anyone deemed a threat to the ideals of the new republic. The guillotine was developed to expedite the mass executions, 2,750 in Paris alone between April 1793 and May 1794. Provincial tribunals executed another 40,000 people during the winter of 1793–1794. It wasn't too long before the Revolution began to consume its own. As one radical supporter of the Revolution was being lead away to Madame Guillotine, she cried, "O Liberty, what crimes are committed in your name."[8] Without a fixed transcendent law and law-giver, law becomes the creation of the State. Any action of the State is justified because the State has supplanted the true God.

The Problem at Nuremberg

After the defeat of Hitler's Third Reich, war crime tribunals were set up in Nuremberg. The purpose, of course, was to judge those who had participated in the grossest of atrocities, the planned extermination of the Jewish race. John Warwick Montgomery explains the problem the tribunal faced:

> When the Charter of the Tribunal, which had been drawn up by the victors, was used by the prosecution, the defendants very logically complained that they were being tried by *ex post facto* laws; and some authorities in the field of international law have severely criticized the allied judges on the same ground.

The most telling defense offered by the accused was that they had simply followed orders or made decisions within the framework of their own legal system, in complete consistency with it, and that they therefore could not rightly be condemned because they deviated from the alien value system of their conquerors. Faced with this argument, Robert H. Jackson, Chief Counsel for the United States at the Trials, was compelled to appeal to permanent values, to moral standards transcending the life-styles of particular societies—in a word, to a "law beyond the law" of individual nations, whether victor or vanquished.[9]

How did the Tribunal account for this "law beyond the law"? What justification was given for its being imposed *ex post facto*? The Tribunal could not appeal to the Bible. Revealed religion had been discounted decades before. Higher Criticism, which had its start in Germany, had effectively destroyed the Bible for so many as a reliable standard for history and law. What about natural law? Sir William Blackstone, whose *Commentaries on the Laws of England* served as the primary foundation of law from the time of the War for Independence to the time of the war between the states, developed a natural law theory based on the doctrine of creation:

> Thus when the supreme being formed the universe, and created matter out of nothing, he impressed certain principles upon that matter, from which it can never depart, and without which it would cease to be.
>
>   * * * * *
>
> This law of nature, being co-eval with mankind and dictated by God himself, is of course superior in obligation to any other. It is binding over all the globe, in all countries, and at all times: no human laws are in validity, if contrary to this; and such of them as are valid derive all their force, and all their authority, mediately or immediately, from this original.
>
>   * * * * *

> Upon these two foundations, the law of nature and the law
> of revelation, depend all human laws; that is to say, no human
> laws should be suffered [permitted] to contradict these.[10]

But with the publication and adoption of Charles Darwin's *On the Origin of Species* in 1859 by the scientific and legal professions, Blackstone's legal worldview was considered to be quaint. Darwinism made natural law a logical impossibility. How could an immaterial law be derived from a purely material cosmos that had come into existence by chance? "Charles Darwin destroyed natural law theory in biological science. . . . His successors destroyed natural law theory in social science. In the 1920's, quantum physics destroyed natural law theory in the subatomic world. This immediately began to undermine modern legal theory."[11] The shattered foundation of natural law theory, like Humpty Dumpty, can never be put together again as long as evolution remains our national religion.[12] At the moment, natural law theory is dead given materialist assumptions that are firmly rooted in every major secular university and law school in the country.

Natural Law on Trial

Does anyone remember how the Senate Judiciary Committee attacked Clarence Thomas for believing that the Constitution had to be interpreted in the light of "natural law"? The Constitution contains little moral prescription. There is no discussion, for example, of what constitutes murder or theft in the body of the Constitution. The Constitution implements whatever moral precepts are generally held by the populace. For example, slavery was practiced in the colonies, and there is no freedom outlined that would give a woman a right to kill her preborn baby. The *Roe v. Wade* decision of 1973 claimed to have found the freedom of abortion in the "penumbra" of the Constitution, an unspecified set of "implied rights."

The framers did not perceive that there was a need to acknowledge a body of law since natural law—"the laws of nature and of nature's

God"—was almost universally accepted. This is why Clarence Thomas could write: "We look at the Natural Law beliefs of the founders as a background to our Constitution."[13] The left-leaning members of the committee took exception to Thomas's natural law beliefs. Joseph Biden wrote an article that appeared in the *Washington Post*[14] in which he claimed the following for his version of natural law:

- It does not "function as being a specific moral code regulating individual behavior."
- It is not "a static set of unchanging principles."
- It is "an evolving body of ideals."

Basically, natural law is whatever the courts say it is. "In our system," Biden writes, "the sole obligation of a Supreme Court justice is to the Constitution. Natural justice can supply one of the important means of understanding the Constitution, but natural law can never be used to reach a decision contrary to a fair reading of the Constitution itself." This is why the Left wants to be the gatekeepers to the Supreme Court by mandating a liberal litmus test to all prospective judges. Biden's article does not tell us anything about how we determine what's right or wrong. Morality is a matter of "individual choice." What happens when two individual choices are in conflict? That's why we need judges.

Biden's concept of "good natural law" as opposed to "bad natural law" does not establish a set of "timeless truths" but rather an evolving body of ideals that changes to permit governments to adjust to new social situations. How convenient. "In short," as Phillip E. Johnson notes, Biden's view of "good natural law doesn't prevent us from doing anything we really want to do."[15] Biden never explains how he derived the content of this good natural law or how to account for any law at all given Darwinian assumptions taught in our schools and mandated by our courts. Of course, even though natural law theory has its problems, it does recognize the existence of a higher law. Ultimately, however, natural law, in order to remain stable, must presuppose the foundation of biblical law.[16]

Who Says?

Some people understood the dilemma of how to account for moral absolutes in a society that officially discounts God. Yale law professor Arthur Leff was perplexed that an agnostic culture even wants enduring values. In a lecture delivered at Duke University in 1979 and published in the *Duke Law Journal,* Leff expressed his bewilderment:

> I want to believe—and so do you—in a complete, transcendent and immanent set of propositions about right and wrong, *findable* rules that authoritatively and unambiguously direct us how to live righteously. I also want to believe--and so do you--in no such thing, but rather that we are wholly free, not only to choose for ourselves what we ought to do, but to decide for ourselves, individual and as a species, what we ought to be. What we want, Heaven help us, is simultaneously to be perfectly ruled and perfectly free, that is, at the same time to discover the right and the good and to create it.[17]

How can a solution ever be found in a random, impersonal cosmos, "governed" (if the word can be used) by chance given Leff's logic? "[W]ith God out of the picture," Johnson writes, "every human being becomes a 'godlet'—with as much authority to set standards as any other godlet or combination of godlets."[18] Any person who utters a moral injunction is most often met with, "Who says? Who are you to impose your morality on me?" Leff continues his logical analysis of the dilemma:

> Putting it that way makes clear that if we are looking for an evaluation, we must actually be looking for an *evaluator*: some machine for the generation of judgments on states of affairs. If the evaluation is to be beyond question, then the evaluator and its evaluative processes must be similarly insulated. If it is to fulfil its role, the evaluator must be the unjudged judge, the unruled legislator, the premise maker who rests on no premises,

the uncreated creator of values. . . . We are never going to get
anywhere (assuming for the moment that there is somewhere to
get) in ethical or legal theory unless we finally face the fact that,
in the Psalmist's words, there is no one like unto the Lord. . . .
The so-called death of God turns out not to have been *His* funeral;
it also seems to have effected the total elimination of any coherent,
or even more-than-momentarily convincing, ethical or legal system
dependant upon final authoritative, extrasystemic premises.[19]

So what is the secularist's answer? How does the modernist create
a moral center in the Darwinian struggle for life? The usual answer is
that "doing good" is what benefits the species. Being kind, for example,
has a good result. But is this always true? The claim is made "that a
variety of widely accepted norms, including the keeping of certain promises, the abhorrence of unjustified killing of human beings, and perhaps
even the sanctity of property rights, promote the adaptation of the human species to its environment. But so does genocide."[20] All the "great"
tyrants claimed that what they did was for the betterment of mankind.
To Hitler, Jews were a world problem. Mass sterilization was first considered, then more efficient and quicker methods were proposed and
carried out to rid the world of the "Jewish problem." But in the end, it
was all done for a "righteous" cause.[21] The Birth Control League founder
Margaret Sanger with her eugenic ideas wanted "to create a race of thor-
oughbreds" by encouraging births of "more children from the fit, and
less from the unfit."[22] She purposely set up birth control clinics in poor
immigrant neighborhoods to rid the world of "mongrel races." Who's
to say, given the presuppositions of today's Darwinian legal theorists,
that any of it was wrong?

While Leff did a masterful job in pointing out the problem, and
he evaluated numerous theories in finding a way out of the dilemma
created by his "own kind," he offered no solution. Even so, people will
continue to maintain, at least for the moment, that napalming babies is
bad, starving the poor is wicked, slavery is evil, war is hell, but there will
always be one lingering question, "Says who?"

Conclusion

Modern legal theory which denies the sovereignty of God over the nations also denies the sovereignty of God over the individual and everything else. When pushed on the point, there is no way to account for anything given Darwinian assumptions, not even reason or logic, the supposed saviors of the rationalist worldview. Christians must face the steamroller effect of this set of assumptions. Laws are being put on the books that when fully implemented and applied will disenfranchise Christians to such an extent that they will not be able to speak the name of Jesus.

Notes

1. Matthew 10:29.

2. Psalm 127:1.

3. George Washington (October 3, 1789).

4. "A Summary View of the Rights of British America," *Thomas Jefferson: Writings* (New York: The Library of America, 1984), 105

5. Jonathan Glover, *Humanity: A Moral History of the Twentieth Century* (New Haven, CT: Yale University Press, 1999), 310.

6. *McGowan v. Maryland*, Supreme Court of the United States, 366 U.S. 420 (May 29, 1961).

7. By referencing "Independence," the framers included the Declaration of Independence which states that we are "endowed by our Creator with certain unalienable rights." The "twelfth" refers to the twelfth year after the drafting of the Declaration: 1776–1787.

8. Denise Dersin, ed., *What Life Was Like During the Age of Reason: France, AD 1600–1800* (Alexandria, VA: Time-Life Books, 1999), 154.

9. John Warwick Montgomery, *The Law Above the Law* (Minneapolis, MN: Dimension Books/Bethany Fellowship, 1975), 24–25.

10. William Blackstone, *Commentaries on the Laws of England*, 4 vols. (Chicago, IL: The University of Chicago Press, [1765–1769] 1979), 1:38, 41, 42.

11. Gary North, *Political Polytheism* (Tyler, TX: Institute for Christian Economics, 1989), xxii.

12. Gary DeMar, "The Religion of Evolution," *Biblical Worldview* (October 2002).

13. "Thomas Spars With Committee over Natural Law and Abortion," *Congressional Quarterly Weekly Review*, 49:38 (September 21, 1991), 2644.

14. Joseph R. Biden, Jr., "Law and Natural Law: Questions for Judge Thomas," *The Washington Post* (September 8, 1991), C-1.

15. Phillip E. Johnson, "The Modernist Impasse in Law," *God and Culture: Essays in Honor of Carl F. H. Henry*, D.A. Carson and John D. Woodbridge, eds. (Grand Rapids, MI: Eerdmans, 1993), 181.

16. Gary DeMar, "The Mating of Biblical Law and Natural Law," *Biblical Worldview* (June 1990).

17. Arthur Leff, "Unspeakable Ethics, Unnatural Law," *Duke Law Journal* (December 1979), 1229–49. Quoted in Johnson, "The Modernist Impasse in Law," 182.

18. Johnson, "The Modernist Impasse in Law," 182.

19. Leff, "Unspeakable Ethics, Unnatural Law." Quoted in Johnson, "The Modernist Impasse in Law," 183.

20. Richard Posner, *The Problems of Jurisprudence* (Boston: Harvard University Press, 1990), 235–236. Quoted in Johnson, "The Modernist Impasse in Law," 184.

21. For a chilling reenactment of the plan, see the HBO Film *Conspiracy: The Meeting at Wannsee*, starring Stanley Tucci, Colin Firth, and David Threlfall. The two-hour meeting on January 20, 1942, essentially sealed the fate of Jews in

Europe. The approach taken by the thirty German bureaucrats was medicinal, a straight forward outline on how to solve the Jewish problem without ever using the words "kill" or "exterminate." The law as it existed in Germany at the time was followed to the letter, giving them proper legal cover and justification for their actions. The date of the meeting nearly coincides with the *Roe v. Wade* decision of 1973 (January 22) which has had a more ominous effect. Safe to say that more than six million Jewish babies have been killed legally through abortion since 1973.

22. Margaret Sanger, *The Pivot of Civilization* (New York: Brentano's, 1922), 126. Quoted in George Grant, *Killer Angel: A Short Biography of Planned Parenthood's Founder, Margaret Sanger*, rev. ed. (Nashville, TN: Cumberland House Publishing, [1995] 2001), 85.

Multiculturalism as Ethical Polytheism

When Joseph A. Fernandez was New York City's School Chancellor, he suspended a school board in Queens because it "adamantly refused to adopt a multicultural curriculum that, among other things, teaches first graders to respect and appreciate gay people."[1] Why this strong opposition to a "multicultural curriculum?"

New Yorkers have lived in ethnic diversity for over a century. New York is one of the most cosmopolitan cities in the world. Most ethnic groups came to New York impoverished with little access to political power. Nearly all ethnic minorities have shared the Harlem zip code. "Harlem was a predominately Jewish community in the early twentieth century."[2] It has only been since the increase of the welfare state that blacks have remained ghettoized in Harlem. While there always have been cultural differences, harmony generally exists among the inhabitants of New York because New Yorkers shared a common ethical heritage. It hasn't always been *West Side Story* and *Gangs of New York*.

While Pittsburgh, Pennsylvania, my hometown, is not as diverse as New York City, it has a similar ethnic mix. On the street where I grew up, there were Italians, Irish, Polish, Ukrainian, Hungarian, and Jews.

So why should these parents in Queens object to a "multicultural curriculum" if there is so much ethnic diversity in their own neighborhoods? Notice the forced connection between multiculturalism and

sexual behavior. Few Americans believe there is such a relationship between multiculturalism and homosexuality. A multicultural curriculum
is not designed to help divergent ethnic groups get along. The modern
curriculum is an imposition of a perverse lifestyle, a worldview that
tolerates any and all behavioral choices.

What made my neighborhood work so well? While we did not all
share the same *ethnic* background, we did share a common *ethical* background. The disintegration of the inner cities is not a result of migrat-
ing ethnic groups. Rather, the disintegration is taking place through the
importation of ethical diversity, a form of ethical polytheism that results in no common and agreed on moral foundation.

Ethical Polytheism

As the Queens' incident indicates, multiculturalism is more than
an appreciation of varied cultural expressions. Multiculturalism is part
of an overall philosophy of life. As it is being framed by social engineers,
multiculturalism is intimately tied to ethics. An appreciation of diverse
cultures is being used as a dodge to smuggle in aberrational moral standards that will have the effect of diluting the impact of biblical Christianity. Multiculturalism is a type of ethical polytheism: many moral
law-orders based on many gods.

Polytheism (all gods are equal) leads to relativism (all moral codes
are equal); relativism leads to humanism (man makes his own laws);
and humanism leads to statism (the State best represents mankind as
the pinnacle of power). As Rushdoony remarks,[3] "because an absolute
law is denied, it means that the only universal law possible is an *imperi-
alistic law*, a law imposed by force and having no validity other than the
coercive imposition."[4]

We are being driven back to the Tower of Babel on the theological
bus of multicultural education: Multiculturalists want to make a name
for *themselves* to displace the name of God. The multiculturalists are
forcing the position, and the word is *forcing*, that all cultures are inherently equal, except, of course, Western culture which does not accept

the view that all cultures are *ethically* equal. Christianity is what makes the difference. Don't think that the multiculturalists don't know this. Biblical Christianity is their ultimate target.

The menace of multiculturalism is not new. God warned the Israelites from mixing with the surrounding nations because of the potential for ethical, not ethnic, pollution. Their separation from the nations was not, as Hal Lindsey suggests, based on racial patterns. "If the Law of Moses were still in force today," Lindsey writes, "there would be no Church, since racial segregation of Israelites from the Gentiles was an essential part of the covenant."[5] There were no *racial* barriers in Israel. The Edomites, for example, had the same ancestry as Israel. Jacob and Esau (Edom) were brothers. They were of the same "race." The Bible tells us that God "made from one [Eve], every nation of mankind to live on all the face of the earth" (Acts 17:26; cf. Gen. 3:20). There can be no racial superiority if one truly believes the Bible. Racism is inherent in evolution, however, the core subject of the public school curriculum. Evolution makes cultural polytheism a reality.

"No Yokes, Please"

The separateness in Israel was over *religious* and *ethical* differences. Israelites were to steer clear of the Canaanites, Hittites, Amorites, Edomites, and Jebusites because of their religious and ethical practices, not because they were different ethnically or racially. A non-Israelite could become a part of the covenant community through circumcision and adherence to the covenant requirements. This would mean denouncing the worldview of paganism. A family could be incorporated into Israel by faith, as was Rahab's family (Joshua 2:8–14).

> Rahab was, from the viewpoint of the Israelites, a foreigner. She did not belong to the chosen people; but through faith she was accepted into their company and enjoyed the privileges and blessings from which formerly she had been excluded. In this she was an exemplification of the truth of the covenant promise

that in the seed of Abraham all the nations of the earth would be blessed (Gen. 22:18; Gal 3:8f). Especially interesting is the fact that, once incorporated into the people of God, she even won an honored place in the line that led to the fulfillment of the divine promises in the birth of Christ. Thus, according to the genealogy at the beginning of Matthew's Gospel, Rahab married Salmon and became the mother of Boaz, who in turn also married an alien woman, Ruth the Moabitess, who became the mother of Obed, David's grandfather (Mt. 1:5f.).[6]

Rahab, a foreigner (Heb. 11:31; James 2:25), and Abraham, an Israelite (Rom. 4:9; James 2:23), are used as examples of Old Testament faith. Rahab abandoned her pagan religion and the ethical system that was inextricably tied to it. Israel was warned "not to follow the customs of the nation which I shall drive out before you," God told them, "for they did all these things, and therefore I have abhorred them" (Leviticus 20:23). Pagan nations were "abhorred" because of their deeds, not because they were of a certain race or nationality.

The New Testament sets up similar religious/ethical barriers. As Christians, we are not to be "bound together with unbelievers," no matter what their ethnic origin (2 Cor. 6:14). Why? "For what partnership have righteousness and lawlessness, or what fellowship has light with darkness? Or what harmony has Christ with Belial, or what has a believer in common with an unbeliever? Or what agreement has the temple of God with idols?" (vv. 14b–16). There is a correlation between worship (Christ vs. Belial) and ethics (righteousness vs. lawlessness). The multiculturalists insist that Belial is as good as Christ, and therefore, righteousness and lawlessness are subjective categories that only have validity within the context of one's accepted belief system. Since we live in what is now a pluralistic society (another name for multiculturalism), claims of right and wrong are only legitimate within the limited parameters of one's worldview. These narrow values have no place in the melting pot of multiculturalism since they would assert that other systems of morality are inherently wrong.

The Need for Mead

The deep descent into the ethical morass of multiculturalism is not new. Its twentieth century prophet was Margaret Mead. If Margaret Mead had not lived, anthropologists would have had to invent her. Mead's *Coming of Age in Samoa* (1928) was the book for which many had "been waiting."[7] Numerous anthropologists were looking for evidence to support what they had concluded *a priori*. But Mead's research, as it turns out, is a myth, an invention to support preconceived ideas of human behavior to justify a freewheeling sexual lifestyle.

At the instigation of Franz Boas, her professor at Columbia University, Margaret Mead embarked on a trip to Samoa where she was to study adolescent behavior. Based on theories of biological determinists, Mead should have found Samoan adolescent behavior paralleling that of America and Europe. Instead, she reported that Samoan "life was easy and casual, and adolescence was the easiest and most pleasant time of life."[8] What did this mean in anthropological terms? "Samoa was a 'negative instance'—and the existence of this one counterexample demonstrated that the disturbances associated with adolescence in the United States and elsewhere had cultural and not biological causes."[9] Thus, Mead gave support to the cultural determinists. (Today, ethicists seem to have moved in the direction of biological determinism—blaming everything from homosexuality to divorce[10] on biology. Biblical Christian holds the doctrine of "original-sin determinism.")

Mead went to Samoa hoping to find empirical support for the presuppositions of her mentor Franz Boas. "Boas maintained that the turmoil among Western youth was more cultural than biological and ascribed its cause, among other things, to repression imposed by the Judeo-Christian ethic on the adolescent's discovery of sexuality."[11] Mead needed to find an unspoiled culture, that is, unspoiled by the influences of Christian missionaries, to test the thesis. Mead reported:

> Romantic love as it occurs in our civilization inextricably
> bound up with ideas of monogamy, exclusiveness, jealousy and

undeviating fidelity does not occur in Samoa. Our attitude is a compound . . . of the institution of monogamy, of the ideas of the age of chivalry, *of the ethics of Christianity.*[12]

Coming of Age in Samoa has been the best-selling of all anthropological books, influencing millions of people, especially college students, throughout the world. Mead's conclusions have cast a long and dark shadow on today's culture, forming, at least implicitly, the foundation of what today is called multiculturalism. Consider some of her conclusions after studying Samoan culture for a few months:

- "Children do not think of an own [*sic*] mother who always protects them," but rather of "a group of adults all of whom have their interests somewhat but not too importantly at heart. . . . The child owes no emotional allegiance to its father and mother."
- Within Samoan culture, claims Mead, each child is "given the means to satisfy his desires completely."
- By the time Mead began her research in Samoa toward the end of 1925, the Manu'ans had all been Christians since the 1840s, and for several generations had taken pride in their adherence to the ordinances of the protestant London Missionary Society. Yet, in the main text of *Coming of Age in Samoa*, Mean makes virtually no reference to the fundamental significance of the Christian church in the day-to-day lives of the Manu'ans. Instead, the place of the Christian religion in Samoa in the mid 1920s is relegated to a single paragraph in an appendix.
- The Samoan's she studied in 1925–1926, despite having been Christian for almost a hundred years, had only, according to Mead, taken such parts of Western culture "as made their life more comfortable, their culture more flexible" and were "without the doctrine of original sin."
- The Samoans, according to Mead, as well as having no conviction of sin, regarded lovemaking as "the pastime *par excellence,*" made "a fine art of sex," and had, of all the people she had

studied, "the sunniest and easiest attitudes towards sex." Samoan society, she reported, "works very smoothly as it is based on the general assumption that sex is play, permissible in all hetero- and homosexual expression, with any sort of variation as an artistic addition."

- "Marriage makes no violent claims for fidelity" and adultery "is not regarded as very serious." Many adulteries occur "which hardly threaten the continuity of established relationships." A man who seduces his neighbor's wife simply has to settle with his neighbor, as "the society is not interested."
- Young females "defer marriage through as many years of casual lovemaking as possible," it being one of their "uniform and satisfying ambitions" to live as girls "with many lovers as long as possible" before marrying and settling down to have many children.
- With "no religious worries," "no conflicts with their parents," and "no confusion about sex" to vex the souls of Samoan girls, their development is "smooth, untroubled, unstressed."

The Myth Becomes Reality

Does any of this sound familiar? Mead's depiction of Samoan culture is pervasive in American culture. Samoan sexual mores, as advocated by Mead, are now America's sexual mores. The Meadian paradigm has become standard fare in movies, television, magazines, music, print advertising, and sex education classes in our nation's government schools. Non-judgmental sexual promiscuity is a right of passage for a majority of teenagers. A school's only goals are to keep teenagers from getting pregnant[13] and acquiring deadly diseases. Homosexuality is accepted as a normal, albeit alternative, lifestyle. Adultery is portrayed as if it has minimal effects on families and society. We need to be more like the carefree Samoans who were not tainted by the idea of original sin, modern-day Meadian prophets tell us. Moral judgments are not to be made.

Margaret Mead's target was biblical Christianity. Her dubious research methods and unsupported conclusions were designed to cause people to question the reality of original sin and the merits of biblical law. Those who praised Mead's thesis understood what she was trying to accomplish. Samuel D. Schmalhausen, an eager advocate of Mead's glowing account of the utopian character of Samoan life, proclaimed her "discoveries" as "a new enlightenment." Derek Freeman describes Schmalhausen's understanding of the implications of Mead's thesis as a "new gospel."

Schmalhausen, convinced by Mead's evidence of what he called "the innocent, strangely impersonal, naively mechanistic-behavioristic sexing of the lighthearted youths and maidens of far-off Samoa," felt there were but "two roads of heart's fulfillment: *Samoa or Calvary*: happy-go-lucky felicity or tragic intensity."[14]

Robert H. Lowie echoed Schmalhausen. He "found Mead's 'graphic picture of Polynesian free love' convincing and, in his review in the *American Anthropologist*, he accepted her major conclusion that the stress and strain characteristic of American adolescents were 'not rooted in original nature' but in the 'repressive agencies' of society." Do you want to guess what Lowie meant by "repressive agencies"?[15]

The cultural determinism Mead said she found among the Samoans is fraudulent. Derek Freeman, who spent many years in Samoa, calls her work a "myth." "Mead's depiction of Samoa are fundamentally in error, and some of them preposterously false," Freeman asserts. "Some Samoans who have read *Coming of Age in Samoa* react . . . with anger and the insistence 'that Mead lied.'"[16] There is "conclusive empirical evidence to demonstrate that Samoa, in numerous respects, is not at all as Mead depicted it to be."[17]

Why did those in the anthropological community so easily embrace Mead's conclusions? They wanted to believe. It allowed them to justify their liberal lifestyles. For example, Bertrand Russell, who had become well known in New York as an advocate of sexual freedom, considered Mead's Samoan account as a justification for adultery.[18]

America has become the society that Margaret Mead fabricated. Teenagers are taught how to perform guilt-free sex, fully protected, of course. Sexual "preference is non-judgmental. If a similar were study were done today, it would have the title, *Coming of Age in America*. Its conclusions, however, would not be mythical.

Notes

1. Steven Lee Myers, "School Board Out in New York," *New York Times* (December 2, 1992), A1.

2. Thomas Sowell, *Ethnic America: A History* (New York: Basic Books, 1981), 95.

3. Rousas J. Rushdoony, *The Institutes of Biblical Law* (The Craig Press, 1973), 17.

4. Gary North, *Political Polytheism* (Tyler, TX: Institute for Christian Economics, 1989), 158.

5. Hal Lindsey, *The Road to Holocaust* (New York: Bantam Books, 1989), 265.

6. Philip Edgcumbe Hughes, *A Commentary on the Epistle to the Hebrews* (Grand Rapids, MI: Eerdmans, 1977), 504.

7. Ruth Benedict, *The New Republic.* Quoted in Derek Freeman, *Margaret Mead and Samoa: The Making and Unmaking of an Anthropological Myth* (Cambridge, MA: Harvard University Press, 1983), 100.

8. Freeman, *Margaret Mead and Samoa*, xi.

9. Freeman, *Margaret Mead and Samoa*, xi-xii.

10. "Genes Are Linked To Divorce," *Fayetteville (North Carolina) Observer-Times* (November 29, 1992), 29A.

11. Ian T. Taylor, *In the Minds of Men: Darwin and the New World Order* (Toronto, Canada: TFE Publishing, 1987), 416.

12. Margaret Mead, *Coming of Age in Samoa* (New York: William Morrow, [1928] 1973), 79.

13. "Frustrated by their apparent inability to put a dent in the city's high teenage pregnancy rate, Baltimore public health officials are planning to offer Norplant, the surgically implanted contraceptive, at clinics in city schools." These promiscuous teenagers are "very interested in a contraceptive that will get them through their school years," said Dr. Peter Beilsenson, city health commissioner. (Tamar Lewin, "Baltimore School Clinics to Offer Birth Control by Surgical Implant," *The New York Times* [December 4, 1992], A1).

14. Freeman, *Margaret Mead and Samoa*, 97. Emphasis added.

15. Freeman, *Margaret Mead and Samoa*, 99.

16. Freeman, *Margaret Mead and Samoa*, 289.

17. Freeman, *Margaret Mead and Samoa*, 292.

18. Freeman, *Margaret Mead and Samoa*, 98.

Conclusion

Recently a historian commented on what he had observed of the Christian faith in America: "Socially irrelevant, even if privately engaging."[1]

Modern-day humanism is dominant in our nation and has set the church of Jesus Christ on the run. We can see the expression of a man-centered philosophy entrenched in the courts, schools, colleges, medical schools, the media, and in Congress. Even the church has been over-run by pagan ideologies. Too often Christians believe that the world is evil and under the control of the devil. These beliefs are not Christian.[2]

One reason for humanism's dominance in today's world is the Christian's preoccupation with retreatism. We have bought the bill of goods humanists have sold us--*that Christians have no business preaching and teaching about topics pertaining to this world.* "Preach about heaven and the return of Jesus Christ, but do not meddle, for example, in the areas of economics, law, politics, and education. These are strictly *secular* matters." As long as churches followed this prescription, Christian individuals, families, and churches were not opposed. *An ineffective church is a tolerated church.*

Because Christians have neglected the world for so long, we have very little media, legal, political, and even religious influence to champion our cause that Jesus is Lord and Savior. The church is experiencing what Israel suffered under the tyranny of the Midianites: "And the power of Midian prevailed against Israel. Because of Midian the sons of Israel *made for themselves the dens which were in the mountains and the caves and the strongholds*" (Judges 6:11). Very little of any long-term dominion can be accomplished when people operate from caves. One's productivity has to be hidden or it will be confiscated (6:11).

The Individual

The restoration of our nation begins with the individual. Only the conversion of many can result in long-term reformation. I assume that you already are a Christian, that you have repented of your sins and have turned to Jesus Christ as your only hope for salvation and are in no way depending on your own so-called "good works" to make you acceptable with God.

You must recognize God as a God of love and justice—two inseparable attributes. Because God loves His people, He sent Jesus, His only Son, to die for their sins. Justice necessitated the death of Jesus. Divine justice had to be satisfied. Peace with *God* (not the devil) had to be made (Rom. 5:1). This message must be preached world-wide. No nation can experience the restoration process without repentance of sin and unconditional surrender to God through Jesus Christ.

Regeneration is only the first step, however. Born again, we are still spiritual infants, babes in Christ: "Like newborn babes, long for the pure milk of the word, that by it you may grow in respect to salvation, if you have tasted the kindness of the Lord" (1 Peter 2:2, 3). Peter tells us there is a growth process. We must not remain "babes." Many Christians never leave infancy, however, but instead resemble the Christians described in the epistle to the Hebrews: "For by this time you ought to be teachers, you have need again for someone to teach you the elementary principles of the oracles of God, and you have come to need milk and not solid food. For every one who partakes only of milk is not accustomed to the word of righteousness, for he is a babe. But solid food is for the mature, who because of practice have their senses trained to discern good and evil" (Heb. 5:12-14).

The restoration process begins with the individual and must be total. Restoration affects body and soul (1 Thess. 5:23; 2 Cor. 5:17; Rom. 6:12-14; 12:1; 1 Cor. 6:15, 20); the mind (Prov. 2:2; John 6:45; Rom. 12:2; Col. 3:1, 2; 1 Peter 1:13); the will (Ezek. 36:25-27; Matt. 7:21; Mark 3:35; Col. 1:9-12, 21); the passions (Gal. 5:24; Col. 3:5-17); and the conscience (Titus 1:15; Heb. 9:14). "Society" possesses no will of its own but reflects the people's will. If "society" is to be restored, individuals must be restored. Christians must understand that the Christian life goes beyond regeneration and justification to discipleship and sanctification. We are held accountable for the "whole purpose of God" (Acts 20:27).

A Steady Diet of God's Word

The Bible, from Genesis to Revelation, must become our steady diet. If we do not know how to "handle accurately the word of truth" (2 Tim. 2:15), we cannot discern the times and offer biblical solutions to personal, family, and societal problems (cf. 1 Chron. 12:32).

Besides a comprehensive biblical education, we must develop an educational program that will cover the world, not just our small corner of it (Isa. 11:9). This means applying what we learn from the Bible to every area of human thought. We should read and study books on economics, politics, education, law, medicine, journalism, foreign policy, ecology, philosophy, agriculture, ethics, psychology, science, and every other God-created sphere of learning. God supplies His people with gifts and talents for building the Kingdom. God requires us to account for our use of those gifts and talents. He does not restore us simply to provide for our private and self-centered use of those gifts.

Christians also must be future-oriented. Decisions made today affect future generations. We cannot give up on this world. Jesus calls us to victory now! Satan was crushed under the feet of the first century Christians (Rom. 16:20), not Jesus.

Why do many Christians act as though Jesus was not raised from the dead? There could be no power in a crucified Jesus who remained in a tomb. Thus, Paul wanted to know the *"power* of His resurrection" (Phil. 3:10). Paul also writes that Jesus is the *"power* of God" (1 Cor. 1:24), the gospel is the *"power* of God for salvation" (Rom. 1:16), and "all *authority* and *power* and *dominion"* belong to Jesus (Eph. 1:21).

Christians should work to rebuild all institutions according to the blueprint laid down in Scripture. Too often we satisfy ourselves with occupying a square foot of living space in the humanists' palace. Tommy Rogers writes:

> We must know our enemy, but we must have a solid base from which to evaluate our position and to assess the enemy. We must learn, first, to direct our efforts at *substance* rather than [solely] symbol. It is not of particular importance to return "prayer" to public schools, or to pass bills requiring "creationism." Why should we be satisfied with so-called "prayer" offered to an unknown god in a humanistically dominated establishment? The overriding issue is to dismantle the public schools, for the whole humanistic system seeks to avoid God.[3]

We fight for crumbs when Jesus tells us to sit and feast. We seem happy for a chance to be heard in the public school classroom when Jesus has given us the world.

It's difficult to swallow the idea that change begins with you and me. What difference can one person make? What difference does one rain drop make in a flood? What difference does one spark make in a forest fire. What difference did Joseph make in Egypt? What difference did Daniel make in Babylon?

God calls on us one by one to conform our lives to the image of His Son. There is no magical formula for change. The standard for righteousness is set forth in Scripture. Just think what would happen if Christians around the world would begin to affect their world where they live. There would be a title wave of change. Those without Christ would want what we have. Our works would be a testimony to our faith. What would your witness do to your neighborhood, your place of work, even your church? The transformation of our world is dependent on the transformation of the body of Christ. It begins with you. It begins with me.

Notes

1. Os Guinness, *The Gravedigger File: Papers on the Subversion of the Modern Church* (Downers Grove, IL: InterVarsity Press, 1983), 79.

2. Gary DeMar, *"You've Heard It Said": Biblical Myths that Neutralize Christians* (Powder Springs, GA: American Vision, 2003).

3. Tommy Rogers, "An Epistemology for Dominion," *Journal of Christian Reconstruction*, Symposium on Social Action, ed. Gary North," 8:1 (Summer 1981), 80.

America's Christian Heritage

"Blessed is the nation whose God is the Lord, the people whom He has chosen for His own inheritance" (Psalm 33:12).

Both religious and political persecution motivated colonists to leave the security of civilization to embark on a mission to carve a "Christian Commonwealth" out of an unknown and hostile wilderness. "The purpose of the New England colonies was, with respect to church and state, twofold: First, to establish the true and free church, free of the *control* of the state, free to be a co-worker in terms of the Kingdom of God, to establish God's Zion on earth, second, to establish godly magistrates, i.e., a Christian state, magistrates as ordained by God."[1] None of these objectives was accomplished without cost.

The separation of Christianity from the workings of the State was not the objective of these early settlers. The following evidence will show that Christianity was the motivating force behind our founders' desires to establish a "city on a hill."[2]

The Early Colonies

Our nation begins, not in 1776, but more than a 160 years earlier in a small outpost called Jamestown (1607). The original charter acknowledged the "providence of Almighty God" and "the glory of His Divine Majesty" to bring the "Christian religion to [those] . . . as yet live in darkness and miserable ignorance of the true knowledge and worship of God."[3] A second colony destined for the "northern parts of Virginia" came with a similar purpose in 1620 as William Bradford (1589–1657) described in his *History of Plymouth Plantation*:

> A great hope and inward zeal they had of laying some good foundation, or at least to make some way thereunto, for the propagating and advancing the Gospel of the Kingdom of Christ in those remote parts of the world; yea, though they should be but even as stepping stones unto others for the performing of so great a work.[4]

The Mayflower Compact was drafted prior to the Pilgrim's arrival in what is now the Cape Cod area of Massachusetts in November of 1620. Because their original charter did not apply to their new landing site, a workable governing document had to be hastily drawn up in order to avoid anarchy. The Compact reads in part:

> **In the name of God, Amen**. We, whose names are underwritten, the loyal subjects of our dread sovereign lord King James, **by the grace of God**, of Great Britain, France, and Ireland, king, defender of the faith, etc., **having undertaken for the glory of God and advancement of the Christian faith**, and the honor of our king and country, a voyage to plant the first colony in the northern parts of Virginia; do by these presents, solemnly and mutually **in the presence of God** and one another, covenant and combine ourselves together into a civil body politic, for our better ordering and preservation and furtherance of other ends aforesaid; and by virtue hereof do enact, constitute and frame such just and equal laws, ordinances, acts, constitutions and offices, from time to time, as shall be thought most [suitable] and convenient for the general good of the colony; unto which we promise all due submission and obedience.[5]

Their voyage was "for the glory of God and advancement of the Christian faith." The Pilgrims understood that all of life was under the sovereign dominion of God. All their pursuits, including the building of homes, churches, and schools and carving out new homes in the wilderness, ultimately would lead to the glory of God.

The Fundamental Orders of Connecticut (1639) reads that "there should be an orderly and decent government established according to God, to order and dispose of the affairs of all the people at all seasons as occasions shall require. . . . [T]o maintain and preserve the liberty and purity of the Gospel of our Lord Jesus which we now profess, as also the discipline of the churches, which according to the truth of the said Gospel is now practiced among us.[6]

The New England Confederation (1643) stated, "Whereas we all came into these parts of America with one and the same end and aim, namely, to advance the Kingdom of our Lord Jesus Christ and to enjoy the liberties of the Gospel in purity with peace; and whereas in our settling (by a wise providence of God) we are further dispersed upon the sea coasts and rivers than was a first intended."[7]

Colleges

One of the first things colonial founders did after building their homes and churches was to establish schools. If a young man wanted to continue his education, he would have to make the arduous and expensive journey back to England. Harvard College (founded in 1636, six years after the arrival of the British Puritans) stated its purpose clearly: "Let every student be plainly instructed, and earnestly pressed to consider well, the main end of his life and studies is, to know God and Jesus Christ which is eternal life (John 17:3) and therefore lay Christ at the bottom, as the only foundation of all sound knowledge and learning." The initiators of Harvard wanted the Puritan legacy to continue: "One of the next things we longed for, and looked after was to advance *Learning* and perpetuate it to Posterity; dreading to leave an illiterate Ministry to the Churches, when our present Ministers shall lie in the Dust."

The original Seal of Columbia University, New York, formerly King's College, was adopted in 1755. Over the head of the seated woman is the (Hebrew) Tetragrammaton, YHVH (*Jehovah*); the Latin motto around her head means "In Thy light we see light" (Psalm 36:10); the Hebrew phrase on the ribbon is *Uri El* ("God is my light"), an allusion to Psalm 27:1; and at the feet of the woman is the New Testament passage commanding Christians to desire the pure milk of God's word (1 Peter 2:1, 2).

To counter the theological drift of Harvard, Yale College was established in 1701. The founders of Yale yearned to return to the Christian foundation first laid at Harvard: "Yale in the early 1700s stated as its primary goal that 'every student shall consider the main end of his study [is] to know God in Jesus Christ and answerably to lead a Godly, sober life.'"[8]

Our founders understood the relationship between a sound education based upon biblical absolutes and the future of the nation. Yale College demanded the same rigorous education as Harvard: "All scholars shall live religious, godly, and blameless lives according to the rules of God's Word, diligently reading the Holy Scriptures, the fountain of light and truth; and constantly attend upon all the duties of religion, both in public and secret."

Almost without exception, American colleges were set up and designed to follow a Christian perspective on learning. In addition to Harvard, Yale, and Columbia (King's College), the mottos of a number of schools that are today thoroughly secular, manifested an understanding of the Christian worldview in their founding:

- The University of California (Berkeley): "Let there be light."
- Johns Hopkins: "The truth will set you free."
- Boston University: "Learning, Virtue, and Piety."
- University of Florida: "In God we Trust."
- Rutgers: "Son of Righteousness shine upon the west also."
- Duke University (Trinity College): "Faith and Learning."

The University of Georgia, founded in 1785, was established to "introduce religion and learned clergy to perform divine worship of God, and to cultivate principles of religion and virtue among our citizens--to lay an early foundation for enduring seminaries of learning." The bylaws of Duke University stated: "The Aims of Duke University are to assert a faith in the eternal union of knowledge and religion set forth in the teachings and character of Jesus Christ, the Son of God."[9]

The influence of these early colleges should not go unnoticed. Church leaders were educated in their classrooms, and civil rulers gained an understanding of the application of biblical law to civil affairs.

Publishing

"The first printing press in the American colonies was set up at Cambridge in 1639, and from it in 1640 issued the first book, THE WHOLE BOOKE OF PSALMES *Faithfully* TRANSLATED *into* ENGLISH *Metre, Whereunto is prefixed a discourse declaring not only the lawfulness, but also the necessity of the heavenly Ordinances of singing Scripture Psalmes in the Churches of God.*"[10]

Kirk House writes that "Cotton Mather . . . [b]orn in 1663, took his M.A. from Harvard at age 18 and joined his father in his Boston pastorate . . . Widely regarded as the most brilliant man in New England, he wrote 450 books and was a Fellow of the Royal Society. Scientist as well as pastor, he successfully introduced smallpox inoculation during the 1721 epidemic, and had his house bombed for his trouble."[11] Mather wrote a history of early New England which he entitled *Magnalia Christi Americana*, or *The Great Achievement of Christ in America*. "The sum of the matter," he explained, "is that from the beginning of the Reformation in the English nation, there had always been a generation of godly men, desirous to pursue the reformation of religion, according to the Word of God. . . ." But in England, there were others with "power . . . in their hands" who desired "not only to stop the progress of the desired reformation but also, with innumerable vexation, to persecute those that most heartily wish well unto it." The Puritans were here "driven to seek a place for the exercise of the Protestant religion, according to the light of conscience, in the deserts of America." Their purpose was nothing less than to complete the Reformation, believing "that the first reformers never intended that what they did should be the absolute boundary of reformation . . . ."[12]

In 1661, a translation of the Bible in the language of the Algonquian Indians became the first Bible printed in America. It was the work of John Eliot (1604–1690), a Puritan who dedicated his life to evangelizing and teaching the Indians and who earned the title "Apostle of the Indians."

The 1777 Committee on Commerce approved the importing of 20,000 copies of the Bible from Scotland, Holland, and elsewhere. Congressmen resolved to pass this proposal because they believed "the use of the Bible is so universal, and its importance so great."[13] Even though the resolution passed, action was never taken to import the Bibles. Instead, Congress began to put emphasis on the printing of Bibles within the United States. In 1777 Robert Aitken of Philadelphia published a New Testament. Three additional editions were published. The 1779 edition was used in schools. Aitken's efforts proved so popular that he announced his desire to publish the whole Bible. He called upon Congress to help:

> *Resolved*, That the United States in Congress assembled, highly approve the pious and laudable undertaking of Mr. Aitken, subservient to the interest of religion as well as the progress of the arts in this country, and being satisfied from the above report, of his care and accuracy in the execution of the work, they commend this edition of the Bible to the inhabitants of the United States, and hereby authorize him to publish this recommendation in the manner he shall think proper.[14]

Given the adversarial relationship between the American Civil Liberties Union and the courts, there is no possible way that such a resolution would pass or even be proposed today.

Official Acts of Congress and Presidents

1. Our nation's currency carries the motto "In God We Trust."[15]

2. The president is authorized to proclaim at least two National Days of Prayer each year.

3. The words "under God" were inserted into the Pledge of Allegiance by an act of Congress in 1954.

4. On April 30, 1863, President Abraham Lincoln appointed a "National Fast Day." It reads in part: "It is the duty of nations as well as of men to own their dependence upon the overruling power of God, to confess their sins and transgressions in humble sorrow yet with assured hope that genuine repentance will lead to mercy and pardon, and to recognize the sublime truth, announced in the Holy Scriptures and proven by all history: that those nations only are blessed whose God is the Lord."[16]

5. Congress declared 1983 to be the "Year of the Bible" which read in part: "The Bible, the Word of God, has made a unique contribution in shaping the United States as a distinctive and blessed nation. . . . Deeply held religious convictions springing from the Holy Scriptures led to the early settlement of our Nation. . . . Biblical teaching inspired concepts of civil government that are contained in our Declaration of Independence and the Constitution of the United States."[17]

6. When the Supreme Court convenes and the chief justice and associate justices stand before their desks, the marshal makes an ascription to Almighty God in the Court Call saying, "God save the United States and this honorable court."

7. The same year that Congress approved adding the phrase "under God" to the Pledge of Allegiance, both houses passed a resolution directing the Capitol architect to make available "a room, with facilities for prayer and meditation, for the use of members of the Senate and House of Representatives."[18]

The history that gives this room its inspirational lift is centered in the stained glass window. George Washington kneeling in prayer . . . is the focus of the composition. . . . Behind Washington a prayer is etched: "Preserve me, O God, for in Thee do I put my trust," the first verse of the sixteenth Psalm. There are upper and lower medallions representing the two sides of the Great Seal of the United States. On these are inscribed the phrases: *annuit coeptis*—"God has favored our undertakings"—and *novus ordo seclorum*—"A new order of the ages is born." Under the upper medallion is the phrase from Lincoln's immortal Gettysburg Address, "This Nation under God.". . . The two lower corners of the window each show the Holy Scriptures, an open book and a candle, signifying the light from God's law, "Thy Word is a lamp unto my feet and a light unto my path" [Psalm 119:105].[19]

The prayer room is decidedly Christian in character. The Bible is featured, not the Book of Mormon, the Koran, or any other religious writings. Religious citations are taken exclusively from the Bible.

Government Buildings, Inscriptions, and Mottos

1. The words "In God We Trust" are inscribed in the House and Senate chambers.

2. On the walls of the Capitol dome, these words appear: "The New Testament according to the Lord and Savior Jesus Christ."

3. In the Rotunda of the Capitol is the figure of the crucified Christ.

4. A painting depicting "The Baptism of Pocahontas at Jamestown" (1613) hangs in the Capitol Rotunda.

5. The "Embarkation of the Pilgrims" shows Elder William Brewster holding a Bible opened to the title page which reads "The New Testament of Our Lord and Savior Jesus Christ." The words "God With Us" are inscribed on the sail of the ship. This painting also hangs in the Rotunda of the Capitol.

6. A relief of Moses hangs in the House Chamber. Moses is surrounded by twenty-two other lawgivers.

7. The Ten Commandments are engraved on the lower half of two large oak doors as you enter the Chamber of the Supreme Court. A marble frieze in the Chamber itself shows Moses holding a copy of the Ten Commandments. Just above the place where the Chief Justice sits, a carved stone banner reads "Justice, the Guardian of Liberty." Centered above the banner, a seated Moses is shown holding a copy of the Ten Commandments.

8. The Latin phrase *Annuit Coeptis*, "[God] has smiled on our undertaking," is inscribed on the Great Seal of the United States.

9. The Liberty Bell has Leviticus 25:10 prominently displayed in a band around its top: "Proclaim liberty throughout all the land, unto the inhabitants thereof."

10. President Eliot of Harvard chose Micah 6:8 for the walls of the Library of Congress: "He hath showed thee, O man, what is good; and what doth God require of thee, but to do justly, and to love mercy, and to walk humbly with thy God."

11. The lawmaker's library quotes the Psalmist's acknowledgment of the beauty and order of creation: "The heavens declare the glory of God, and the firmament showeth His handiwork" (Psalm 19:1).

12. Engraved on the metal cap on the top of the Washington Monument are the words: "Praise be to God." Lining the walls of the stairwell are numerous Bible verses: "Search the Scriptures" (John 5:39), "Holiness to the Lord," and "Train up a child in the way he should go, and when he is old he will not depart from it" (Prov. 22:6).

13. The crier who opens each session of the Supreme Court closes with the words, "God save the United States and the Honorable Court."

14. At the opposite end of the Lincoln memorial, words and phrases from Lincoln's Second Inaugural Address allude to "God," the "Bible," "providence," "the Almighty," and "divine attributes."

15. A plaque in the Dirksen Office Building has the words "IN GOD WE TRUST" in bronze relief.

16. The Jefferson Memorial includes these words from Thomas Jefferson: "God who gave us life gave us liberty. Can the liberties of a nation be secure when we have removed a conviction that these liberties

are the gift of God? Indeed I tremble for my country when I reflect that God is just, that his justice cannot sleep forever."[20]

17. Each president, with the exception of Thomas Jefferson, has taken the presidential oath with his left hand placed on an open Bible while affirming "So help me God." The bronze Senate Doors show George Washington taking the presidential oath with his hands on an open Bible.

19. State mottos: Arizona ("God Enriches"), Florida ("In God We Trust"), Ohio ("With God all Things are Possible"), and South Dakota ("Under God, the People Rule").

20. The Constitution sets Sunday aside as a day of rest for the President (*Art. 1, sec. 7*).

Court Decisions

In 1892, the United States Supreme Court determined, in the case *The Church of the Holy Trinity vs. United States*, that America was a Christian nation from its earliest days. The court opinion, delivered by Justice David Brewer, was an exhaustive study of the historical and legal evidence documenting America's Christian heritage. After examining hundreds of court cases, state constitutions, and other historical sources, the court came to the following conclusion:

> Our laws and our institutions must necessarily be based upon and embody the teachings of the Redeemer of mankind. It is impossible that it should be otherwise; and in this sense and to this extent our civilization and our institutions are emphatically Christian. . . . This is a religious people. This is historically true. From the discovery of this continent to the present hour, there is a single voice making this affirmation . . . . We find everywhere a clear recognition of the same truth . . . . These, and many other matters which might be noticed, add a volume of unofficial declarations to the mass of organic utterances that this is a Christian nation.[21]

In his book *The United States: A Christian Nation*, published in 1905, Brewer came reinforced his earlier study as as Supreme Court Justice with this assessment: "This is a Christian nation."[22]

Our National Anthem

"The Star Spangled Banner," which was a poem penned by Francis Scott Key on September 14, 1814, became our national anthem by an act of Congress in 1931. Our national motto, "In God We Trust, is taken from a line in the anthem which includes the phrase "In God is our trust":

> Oh thus be it e're when free men shall stand
> Between their lov'd homes and war's desolation.
> Blest with the victory and peace, may
> the heav'n rescued land
> Praise the Pow'r that hath made
> and preserved us a nation!
> Then conquer we must,
> when our cause it is just,
> And this be our motto "In God is our Trust."
> And the Star-Spangled banner in triumph shall wave
> O'er the land of the free and the home of the brave.

The Constitution

Michael Newdow, an atheist who went to court to have "under God" removed from the Pledge of Allegiance, has moved his legal fight to remove "In God We Trust" from our nation's currency. Newdow claims that there is "something in the Constitution that says you're not allowed to do that." Actually, there is no such constitutional prohibition. The Constitution itself acknowledges the lordship of Jesus Christ just above where the signatories placed their names on the document: "DONE in Convention by the Unanimous Consent of the States present the Seventeenth Day of September *in the Year of our Lord* one thousand seven hundred and Eighty seven and of the Independence of the United States of America the Twelfth."[23]

Conclusion

The first basic principle in the biblical blueprint for government is that the foundation upon which a nation is built is a reflection of the god that the nation worships.

Our forefathers understood that, as is evident in the words of Benjamin Franklin, "God governs in the affairs of men." Any people that refuses to acknowledge that God must be set as the "chief cornerstone" in all attempts to build a nation, including the United States, will succeed no better than the builders of Babel.

The rich Christian heritage of America is evidence that we began as a Christian nation, that God is truly the "ruler of the kings of the earth." Any nation that rejects God as its sovereign will be broken "with a rod of iron" and will certainly "perish in the way" (Psakm 2:9, 12).

Libraries are filled with the histories of men and nations who sought to overrule the "King of kings and Lord of lords" (Rev. 19:15). There is no hope for those who "take counsel together against the LORD and against His Anointed" (Psalm 2:2).

Notes

1. Rousas J. Rushdoony, *This Independent Republic: Studies in the Nature and Meaning of American History* (Nutley, NJ: The Craig Press, 1964), 97-98.

2. Expanded versions of this historical material can be found in Gary DeMar, *America's Christian History: The Untold Story*, 2nd ed. (Powder Springs, GA: American Vision, 1995) and *America's Christian Heritage* (Nashville, TN: Broadman & Holman, 2003).

3. "First Charter of Virginia" (April 10, 1606), *Documents of American History*, ed. Henry Steel Commager, 6th ed. (New York: Appleton-Century-Crofts, 1958), 8.

4. William Bradford, *History of Plymouth Plantation: 1606-1646*, ed. William T. Davis (New York: Charles Scribner's Sons, 1908), 46.

5. William Bradford, "Mayflower Compact," *History of Plymouth Plantation*, 106-107.

6. "Fundamental Orders of Connecticut" (January 14, 1639), *Documents*, 23.

7. "The New England Confederation" (May 19, 1643), *Documents*, 26.

8. William C. Ringenberg, *The Christian College: A History of Protestant Higher Education in America* (Grand Rapids, MI: William B. Eerdmans Publishing Co., 1984), 38.

9. Quoted in George M. Marsden, *The Soul of the American University: From Protestant Establishment to Established Nonbelief* (New York: Oxford University Press, 1994), 322.

10. Sydney E. Ahlstrom, *A Religious History of the American People* (New Haven, CT: Yale University Press, 1972), 149—150.

11. Kirk House, *God's Claims on Your Children: Readings in the Last 2000 Years of Christian Education* (Sterling, VA: GAM Printers, 1977), 61.

12. *The Modern Age: The History of the World in Christian Perspective* (Pensacola, FL: A Beka Book Publications, 1981), 241.

13. From a report submitted to Congress, quoted in John Wright, *Early Bibles in America*, 3rd rev. ed. (New York: Thomas Whittaker, 1894), 55.

14. Quoted in Wright, *Early Bibles in America*, 58.

15. Stokes and Pfeiffer, *Church and State in the United States*, 570. Complete information can be found online at www.ustreas.gov/opc/opc0011.html.

16. Abraham Lincoln, "Proclamation Appointing a National Fast Day," April 30, 1863, *The Collected Works of Abraham Lincoln*, ed. Roy P. Bassler (New Brunswick, NJ: Rutgers University Press, 1953), 6:155-56.

17. Public Law 97-280, 96 Stat. 1211, approved October 4, 1982.

18. "The Prayer Room of the United States Capitol," booklet published by the U.S. Printing Office, 1956.

19. *The Capitol* (Washington DC: United States Government Printing Office, 1979), 24-25.

20. The inscription that appears on the Jefferson Memorial are a composite of several of Jefferson's writings, some of which are taken out of context. (James W.

Loewen, *Lies Across America: What Our Historic Sites Get Wrong* [New York: The New Press, 1999], 327–332).

21. For a comprehensive study of the Christian foundation of America, see Gary DeMar, *America's Christian History: The Untold Story*, 2nd ed. (Powder Springs, GA: American Vision, 2000) and *America's Christian Heritage* (Nashville, TN: Broadman & Holman, 2003).

22. David J. Brewer, *The United States: A Christian Nation* (Powder Springs, GA: American Vision, [1905] 1996);

23. "The Twelfth" is a reference to twelve years, beginning with the signing of the Declaration of Independence in 1776 and including when the Constitution was drafted in 1787.